I am loved

You are loved.

Claudette

It is a privilege to be able to recommend Claudette Schlitter to you. From the first time I heard Claudette sing until only recently reading a manuscript of her book I have been totally inspired. Claudette is a living example of the grace of God and I know she will inspire others to realize that there is more if you reach for it. Claudette sings with an anointing that brings about a victory in those she ministers to. She is a perfect example of how when we put our experiences in life into the hands of Almighty God things do change and sweet music will flow.

Pastor Calvin Allcoat, Comber Christian Centre, N. Ireland

This is a beautifully written and very moving life story. Claudette provides great insight into the reasons why people develop eating disorders. Her journey to recovery and healing, together with her witness are inspiring and will be of help to many.

Jane Smith, Director of Anorexia and Bulimia Care

The first time I met Claudette she was singing. It was obvious from the few lines of 'Amazing Grace', which she sang unaccompanied, that she was gifted with a voice of exceptional quality. I'm so glad she has gone on to share her anointed voice with the nation and the world, through her recordings and concerts. And now, as she shares her story too I know many will be blessed and encouraged.

Steven Jenkins, College Dean, Mattersey Hall Christian College

"This is a tight military procedural for fans looking for something like Tom Clancy's Jack Ryan transported to space, with rockets flying, ruthless Russians scheming, and unvarnished trust in the American way." **Library Journal**

SUBORBITAL 7

John Shirley

Lieutenant Art Burkett, US Rangers Airborne, is called up to take part in an urgent rescue mission, using an innovative insertion from orbit. Three scientists have been kidnapped by the terrorist group Thieves in Law and their combined knowledge could result in worldwide devastation.

The rescue is swift but violent. Art and his team return to SubOrbital 7, the military space-plane they landed in, intending to return to safety with hostages rescued and prisoners in tow. But Thieves in Law are not the only people looking for SubOrbital 7 and its occupants. With casualties onboard the orbiting craft and a dwindling oxygen supply, Art and his team must fight an ever-growing threat before time runs out for them, and possibly for the rest of the world.

ALCON
PUBLISHING

For more fantastic fiction, author events,
exclusive excerpts, competitions, limited editions and more

VISIT OUR WEBSITE
titanbooks.com

LIKE US ON FACEBOOK
facebook.com/titanbooks

FOLLOW US ON TWITTER AND INSTAGRAM
@TitanBooks

EMAIL US
readerfeedback@titanemail.com

I am loved

The Poignant Story of an Unloved Girl Who
Found Extraordinary Love

Claudette Schlitter

Authentic

18 17 16 15 14 13 12   7 6 5 4 3 2 1

First published 2012 by Authentic Media Limited
52 Presley Way, Crownhill, Milton Keynes, MK8 0ES.
www.authenticmedia.co.uk

British Library Cataloguing in Publication Data
A catalogue record for this book is available from the
British Library.
ISBN 978-1-86024-860-3

Cover design by David McNeill at Revo Creative (www.revocreative.co.uk).
Cover photo by Ashley Carr Photography(www.ashley-carr.co.uk).
Hair by Tanya Elaine Hairdressing(www.tanyaelainehairdressing.co.uk).

Printed and bound by CPI Group (UK) Ltd, Croydon, CR0 4YY.

For Michael, Chloe and Joshua.
Thank you for loving me.

Contents

Acknowledgements   ix

Prologue   xi

SPRING   1

   Poem: Walls   2

1. The Early Years   3
2. Awakenings   11
3. It's Getting Cold Out There . . .   26
4. Colder and Tougher Still   41

SUMMER   55

   Poem: Musical Dream   56

5. Uncomfortable Heat   57
6. Mad About The Boy   69
7. Lost in Music   84
8. Sunday's Child?   100
9. Me, Myself, and I   114

AUTUMN   125

   Poem: Trust   126

10. The Leaves Are Turning   127
11. The Fatherhood of God   144
12. A Love Too Far   153
13. It Started With a Kiss   169
14. The Vacillating Heart   181
15. Falling Leaves   193

WINTER 211

   Poem: Tears 212

16. A Season of Singing 215

17. The Settling Frost 232

18. Bleak Mid-Winter 248

A WOMAN FOR ALL SEASONS 265

   Poem: The Room 266

19. The Real Me 267

20. I Am Loved 282

   Poem: Call Me Loved 299

   Useful Organizations 300

Acknowledgements

First of all I must thank my beautiful children, Chloe and Joshua, and my husband Michael. You've been patient and encouraging, and I couldn't have done it without you. I also thank my mother who has helped to look after me in every sickness I've had.

Thanks too to Mike and Dee Davis of BlackClover Events and Music Limited. Words are not enough really. We came together at the worst time in my life and it was your encouragement that spurred me on to keep writing, singing and loving. Our family loves your family so much.

I'd also like to thank Greta Sheppard, who not only graciously allowed me to use the extract from her message but upon my contacting her continued to encourage me – a true inspiration. Thanks also to Ish (Ishmael aka Ian Smale), for kind permission to use his song 'Father God'.

Prologue

The Compliment

One morning as I walked by my daughter Chloe's room, I caught a glimpse of her as she was getting ready for church. Now, I know that I am her mother, and by default that means I am biased, but – as we say in Birmingham – 'My g'yal is da bomb.' She really is beautiful. Anyhow, she was at the end of her amazingly long beauty ritual of primping and preening, as is the way of every teenager. She was fixing her hair for the umpteenth time and adding the finishing touches to her outfit, and as I passed by I stopped to gaze on that special teen talent, the ability to get ready as slowly as possible on a Sunday morning. It never ceases to amaze me how teenagers move at a snail's pace even though everyone else – mainly me – is rushing around like mad, preparing dinner, slapping on the bare minimum of make-up and covering myself with perfume to cover the smell of the chicken that I have just smothered in garlic. She was nearly ready, so that morning, instead of telling her to get a move on, I felt the urge to tell her how lovely she looked, so I popped my head around the doorway.

'Do you know that you are beautiful?' I said, not really expecting a response.

She smiled at me with that gorgeous little Colgate smile of hers and replied with great humility, and just a tiny smidgeon of confidence, 'Thanks Mom, I know.'

Then she duly returned the compliment and told me that I was beautiful too. And what do you think was my response? Was it the same demure, composed reaction as my 13-year-old beauty? I wish I could say it was, but it was not. I stood before my child and gave my obligatory moan about my weight, hips, big butt, blotchy skin and my thick hair. I critiqued myself so severely that she gave me a look of sharp disapproval, and then my child, a young slip of a girl with no experience of life and the face of a mere babe, shook her head like the wise woman she is and issued a reproof.

'Gosh Mom! Why do you always have to be so negative? Why can't you just take the compliment? You're beautiful. Can't you just accept it?'

Well, you could have knocked me back with a feather. She is not the kind of girl to speak rudely to anyone let alone her mother, although she can be a little cheeky at times, but her rebuke was deserved. I have to admit that it gave me a wave of pleasure and pain all at the same time. The pleasure was in knowing that she was confident in her own image and had no qualms or hang-ups about herself. The pain was in realizing that I could not say the same for me. That was the day it dawned on me that at such a tender age my child understood something that, in my late thirties, I was yet to learn – how to love myself.

How come after all this time I am still unable to look in the mirror and say, 'I love me'?

It was bad enough that I could not accept the compliment, but worse than that was that I did not know why. What was it that had happened to make me unable to accept praise? In fact, every time someone made an admiring comment, even if it was my husband, I would shuffle uncomfortably and find something negative to point out to them. I suppose we have all done that to some extent, and there is something distinctly British about being self-deprecating, but I knew that what I felt was not right, and it was that morning that my quest began.

Journalling

Throughout my adult life I have written a journal, or I should say journals, as there are many books. Following my daughter's comment I decided to go right back to my first journal entries made at the age of 18 and read through them to see what I thought back when I myself was a teenager. I settled down on my bed that evening with a hot chocolate and copious biscuits, and examined the script. However, by the time I had finished reading the first few years' worth of entries I was overwhelmed by what was contained within the scruffily written pages.

When I began writing my journals I had wanted them to be a true account of my journey. I intended them to be something that I could one day pass on to my children as a reminder of their mother, a lasting inheritance through which they could see how I lived my life, and how much I loved them. The only problem was that what I read was full of depression, feelings of failure and intense sadness. As I continued to browse the painful prose, one persistent and pointed question kept arising:

'Why, when I had been surrounded by the love of my family, friends and church, did I feel unloved?'

I only seemed to write in my journals when I was feeling low, and wondered if maybe I had forgotten to include the good times because I was too busy enjoying them. I didn't know. I did know I needed to redress the balance and tell the full story, and to include the good times along with the bad.

A Book for You

I had thought of another title for this book, which was *Letters to God*, for that is what my journal entries are, but that title was taken. Then I thought of another, *Real Women Eat Chocolate*, but I thought better of it as I suppose fake women do too – oh, you know what I mean!

Jokes aside, as you read this book you might be on your own journey of self-discovery just as I was. Please note that this is not a self-help book in any way, shape, or form, or even a didactic thesis on the attributes of the Proverbs 31 woman who is presented as the perfect wife. (Which, I hasten to add, I have heard preached and 'teached' – to use church vernacular – to death, leaving me feeling completely inadequate in comparison to the woman who gets up early, does everything, is called blessed by everyone, and looks 'fabulous darling' in purple.) No, I am not going to go there but, that being said, my faith is real and very important to me. It is my life source and my love source, and although you may not share the same beliefs I have this book is still relevant, for it is about love and that can only be a good thing.

This book is simply my story, and in it I have put my life, my poetry and my thoughts. It is just me, plain and simple, warts and all. I do not have all the answers, and I got it wrong many times, but I am real. A real person messes up, they doubt, they fear, they hate and they love, and that is what I have written about.

You might see in my story some parallels in your own life, and perhaps you have gone through some of the things I went through, or much worse. You may have felt unloved through childhood neglect or bullying. It could have happened in your adult life through bad relationships, abuse, rejection or betrayal; the list is endless. There are countless factors that can bring a person to a point of self-loathing and hatred of themselves, others and life itself.

You may have experienced one particular situation, something so drastic and devastating that it caused you to close in and build a wall of protection around your heart, making you pledge never to let anyone hurt you in that way again. Alternatively, it could be that life has thrown you blow after blow to the point where it isn't that you refuse to love again, you honestly just don't know how. If this resonates with you then I encourage you to read on, as this book is for you.

A note from the author

This story is about me and I am aware that it is from my perspective. Others may see the way things happened differently, but I can only see and recall the events through my eyes, so their telling will be influenced by my feelings. The darker incidents are written only so that my full journey can be told and understood. They are not intended as a tool to wreak some kind of literary revenge, and for this reason many names have been changed to shield the identities of those who have long been forgiven.

Spring

Walls

Life is a room without walls,
An open space with no doors.
An entrance and an exit awaits,
And all through life there are stairs and gates.

My life is a room with paper walls,
A dream, a song, a note, a scrawl.
And in my room I contemplate,
The possibilities of my fate.

1
The Early Years

But the child who is born on the Sabbath Day, is bonny and blithe and good and gay.

Traditional nursery rhyme

I was born on Sunday 21 November 1971. I was a bonny child, with folds of lumpy fat hiding the dimples that would later mark me out as the girl with the smile. I was the last of my mother's children, but I had a different father to my brothers and sisters. He had numerous children from different women. He left each one as soon as children came into the equation and did the same with my mother too.

I have few memories of my very early years, but still two linger in my mind. At the age of 3 or 4 I began to experience something. Psychologists probably have a name for it and could no doubt explain it all away. Spiritualists or Christians may have another name for it, I don't know, but the fact that I remember it seems significant to me. Night after night I would wake up feeling something nibbling at my feet and when I looked down I saw a fish biting my toes. I would scream and cry as it looked very real to me and when it began to appear in the daytime, at the table as I was eating or when I was playing, I would scream with terror to my mother.

'The fish, the fish!'

There then came a second apparition, and this one would appear only in the dark. At night when I went to sleep a large eye became visible in the top right-hand corner of my mother's bedroom. It would materialize there and only there. I suppose from then I was marked out for special attention from my mother as she sought treatment for me. I was referred to a psychologist for help, but I don't think it proved useful. All I know is that one day, just as these two images had appeared, they disappeared suddenly. Apparently I was heard shouting at them to leave me alone, and they did, but as a result I was left with an extreme fear of the dark. From then on I always had to sleep with the lights on and didn't like going out at night just in case they came back.

Home Life

I was a typical youngest child, spoilt and unaware of the privilege in which I was living by benefiting from the paths forged by my siblings. There was a seventeen-year difference between my eldest brother and me, and the household was divided figuratively into two camps: the older bunch – Indie, Art, Pearl and Troy – and then the kids.

Whenever the term 'the kids' was used by anyone we knew it referred to the three younger children – Serene, Special and me – and, as we only had a two-year age gap between each of us, we naturally stuck together. Home life was as every young child perceives it to be – normal, for it was our home and our life, and I loved it. As a single parent, my mother would go to her cleaning job and work tirelessly from early morning until around five o'clock. The older siblings looked after the younger ones, our mother having got up in the dawn hours to cook dinner before she left for work, which my sister Pearl, the eldest girl, would warm up later.

Although Sunday's child may have been gay in the happy sense of the word, the day that brought out smiles all around was Saturday. It was one of those days when the family came together and worked in harmony cleaning the house, laughing, singing and dancing with each other. We all had our allotted chores and mine was cleaning the wood-work, although I moaned about that a lot, knowing my mother would go easy on me as I was the youngest child. The accompanying soundtrack to our work was the true highlight of our day. The music matched every cleaning motion, and the collection was as impressive as it was eclectic. The family listened to all types and genres; reggae, soul, country and western, rock and roll and of course gospel would blast from the living room stereo. From Tammy Wynette, Elvis and Tom Jones to Bob Marley and the Wailers, Jimmy Cliff, Peter Tosh, Black Uhuru and Birmingham's own Steel Pulse, all grooves and beats pounded the soundtrack to our Saturdays. The wide open windows provided a musical announcement to all that we were home and, most importantly, we were together.

My mother would take both my hands in hers and we'd dance around the living room, swaying to the rolling rhythms of song. I would sing along with all the wrong words, of course, but try to hit the right notes. Singing was in my blood from those early days as we sang to each other. The kids usually ended up putting on Sister Sledge, which signalled an end to our housework as we gave choreographed performances of 'We are Family', 'Lost in Music' and more to our mother who delighted in watching our interpretive dance routines with an expression of joy and sadness. I understood the joy but not the sadness, and it wasn't until I became a mother myself that I think I knew why. Those were precious times that a mother never wants to come to an end, and having older children she must have known that we too would soon mature and no longer delight in the dances of our Saturdays. Those days were a delight, for as we cleaned the house the world seemed full of domestic harmony, song . . . and good food.

On Saturdays our mother would get up early in the morning and cook a full breakfast of fried dumplings, bacon, sausages, eggs, baked beans and a tin of Heinz spaghetti hoops for me. We would all dive in, with even the neighbour's children coming over and sitting at the table expecting to be fed. It was the only day of the week that we would all be around to sit together to eat. I would fight to get the last dumpling so that I could dip it into the sauce of the spaghetti, although I rarely got it as the older ones were always too quick. By the afternoon it was time to get the Saturday Soup ready, with yet more dumplings – this time boiled. The soup contained hard soul food including yam, sweet potato, mutton, pumpkin and cassava. My favourite bit was the packet of Knorr chicken noodle soup that was stirred into the pot to add a bit of flavour. I used to try to get a bowl that was almost completely full to the brim with noodles and nothing else.

Each day of the week had its own culinary delights and we rarely veered from the set menu. On Sundays it had to be rice and peas with fried chicken, coleslaw and macaroni cheese, or cheese and potato pie for the younger children. Monday was leftover day, which usually meant the rice was a bit burned from the bottom of the pot. For some reason on Tuesdays we always had fish, whether from a tin, fresh or salted. My favourite was the rare times we had flying fish; when wrapped in banana leaves and stuffed with herbs from the jar my mother had managed to bring over from her trips back home to Barbados, they were absolutely gorgeous. Each fish meal had the same side dishes: yam, green bananas, cassava or breadfruit with boiled cornmeal dumplings. Whenever we had saltfish and ackee, I would eat the ackee and nothing else.

By midweek the subject of food became a battleground as I gave my mother no end of difficulty when she tried to get me to eat the food of my culture. Wednesday's menu contained meat in some form, usually a lamb or pork chop. It was fatty and gristly because we couldn't afford the more expensive lean cuts of meat, and worse still, if times were hard (and they were hard very often) we would have fried tinned corned beef. This of all the menus was my least favourite meal as the mushy meat would be fried in Stork margarine and topped with onions and tomatoes. On Thursdays we would have a mixed menu that usually consisted of a mishmash and hotchpotch of the week's foods, and I would give my mother grief until she resorted to warming a tin of spaghetti or ravioli, because by then I would refuse to eat.

Friday's dinner, however, was the meal that I waited for, the one I relished and ate with glee – fish and chips from the chip shop. From this I thoroughly earned the title of the English Pickney (pickney meaning 'small child' in West Indian patois), and the more I refused to eat the 'hard food' of my heritage the more spoiled I became, as Mom indulged her little one who was having nightmares. I will never deny that there are some distinct privileges in being the youngest.

Now I am older I adore the food of my youth, but at the time I could not appreciate its beauty, flavour, or the ingenuity of necessity. Why am I going on about food so much, you might ask? Well, food is very important in my life story. You will find out later that I didn't just eat to live, but I soon learned to live to eat.

The First Call – Buds of Faith

Our mother followed the habit of quite a few West Indians back then, which was that even if they themselves didn't go to church they made sure their children did. We were sent to the local Baptist church and we went out of duty and under duress. I don't remember enjoying it much, as the pews were B.C. – by that I mean they gave us 'Botty Cramp', which was one of our favourite sayings. The seats were beautiful solid wood but we could not appreciate the quality. Sitting on those hard, unforgiving benches for hours on end would cause us to lose all sensation in our behinds and, being young, fidgety and somewhat feisty children, we found it not only boring but also very uncomfortable. The quiet and austere meetings were a stark contrast to the joyous, musical Saturdays that preceded these dull Sundays, so when a friend of the family invited us to a new church, we pleaded with our mother to let us try it.

Our first visit to Hockley Pentecostal Church was wonderful because they had something that the other Sunday school did not – sweets and stickers. It was a certain 'child catcher' ploy that could have come straight out of *Chitty Chitty Bang Bang* and we were hooked. They even tempted us further by offering us the chance of winning a prize of our own children's Bible if we continued to attend, and when the leader held up the exemplar and flicked through its pages I was blown away. All the Bibles I had seen before then were black leather-bound tomes or hardback with lots of writing and no pictures at all, but this was different. It was beautiful, with illustrations and cartoons, and was in colour as well. The thought of having my own was too much for my little heart to bear and the overt bribery worked. My sisters and I were smitten. After our first session we kids told our mother about the new fun church that we wanted to go to, and sure enough she allowed us to go there instead. Of course, the people talked about the Bible and Jesus just as in my old Sunday school, but I have to say the incentive of sweets made everything sound new. Even the church building had been renovated so, in comparison to our old Sunday school, we were in heaven. Their pews were cushioned and one could sit on them for at least a couple of hours without feeling that sense of numbness that accompanied our previous Sunday school lessons.

The Sunday school and church were run by two women, Sister Harriet Fisher and Sister Olive Reeve. During the Second World War they had wanted to travel as missionaries, but when the onset of war prevented them from doing so they later found that the mission field they had wanted to go to came to them. The influx from the colonies brought children from around the world to a tiny place in the city centre and Hockley Mission was born. Out of that came a church, and although being traditionalists they never preached or called themselves pastors, they led the church and the Sunday school with a passion about their faith that was revolutionary. I had never heard anyone talk about Jesus the way they did, and they spoke of him as if he were actually alive and not just some distant figure in Bible stories of old.

I remember being 5 years old when I heard Sister Fisher saying that Jesus could be my friend, and the idea that he was not only the God that I was supposed to revere and worship but that he could be a friend as well was a revelation. Week after week I heard the stories from the Bible come alive until one Sunday, when Sister Fisher asked if any of us wanted to have Jesus in our hearts to be our personal friend, I put up my hand in the air instantly and opened the first buds of faith. I knew from the first time I answered his call that I was to follow God for the rest of my life, but what I didn't know was just how hard that was going to be.

2
Awakenings

Oh, my anguish, my anguish! I writhe in pain. Oh, the agony of my heart!
My heart pounds within me, I cannot keep silent . . .

Jeremiah 4:19

The kids in the family were the best of friends, and my two immediate sisters had unique qualities that I admired intensely. An imaginative storyteller, Serene would make up vivid tales to tell us each night. Special, the middle child of 'the kids', was a true beauty with soft, long hair and large, doe-like brown eyes. She also had something that I would envy later in life: she was slim. She might have said she was too slim, but I envied her physique and personality as she was a firecracker of a child who lit up the room when she entered it. Wherever Special went I followed as her darker, chubbier, shadow. I loved copying everything she did. She would give orders and boss me around, and I would comply happily. As the youngest child I looked up to all my siblings, but most of all to her, and although I did not share the same father as my brothers and sisters I didn't feel different or separate. At home we all had no father, but we had our mother – and she was all we needed and wanted.

I was a loved and happy child, full of exuberance, vying for the attention of a mother who worked hard and indulged us as much as she could. I remember when she used to come in from work, we would run to her with hugs and kisses and raid her pockets looking for Opal Fruits and Fox's Glacier Mints. Back then I never noticed how she only had one for each of us. I now appreciate that she was trying to make the packets she bought last as long as possible because money was in short supply, but she still made sure that we never went without even the smallest of treats.

Different Strokes

I paint an idyllic childhood and, through my baby eyes, it was. It was only as I got older that I felt a difference between myself and my siblings, not that they treated me any differently, but the mind can play tricks on even the most secure of children. I remember watching the 1980s American sitcom *Different Strokes* on television and laughing at the characters that were trying to assimilate into a regular family whilst all the while being from completely different worlds. My life was to turn out similar in some respects, for I was always trying to fit in where I wasn't sure I belonged. This was most obvious when I would visit my siblings' grandmother. It was then that the difference could be seen; it was only little things, but it gave me the first taste of my separateness.

Whenever we went to see her, at the end of our visits, even though I would get the same hug as the other children and called her Granny just as they did, I noticed that she would give the other kids twenty or fifty pence pocket money and offer me ten pence. It was insignificantly minor, and shouldn't have mattered, but I began to wonder why. She looked after me as well as she did them, and was kind to me, but somehow this trivial difference seemed to signify something that I had not thought about before – that although I was family, I was not quite her family, not completely, and maybe I wasn't theirs either.

When I was around 7 years old I began to notice this more when cricketing trips and days out were arranged for my siblings with their father and I wasn't allowed to go. My mother said that it was because I was too young, and I'm sure it was, but I started to wonder if it was because I didn't have the same father as them. He wasn't my father and maybe he didn't want me along because of that. It wasn't true, but this is what I thought at the time as my young mind could not understand the complexities of life and relationships. In the end I put aside those minuscule differences and, apart from when they occurred, I felt and was no different to the rest of my family. We were one and the same and we were loved by our mother.

Yet I did have a father of my own who was present in my life. He was a man of substance, and by that I do not mean quality, just quantity, as he had money, pride and arrogance in equally large proportions. My father was a short, rotund man; a black version of Father Christmas in my childhood eyes – always jolly and very popular. This was partly because he owned a vibrant barbershop in the local area where he knew everyone and everyone knew him. A portly, dark man, balding on top, with a neatly trimmed tuft of a goatee beard adding style to a round warm face, he was always crisply dressed in the finest tailored suits. He had countless, expensive trilby hats and he 'cut a dash' in the seventies when most people were becoming more relaxed in their apparel. When I think of it now he probably looked like the stereotypical pimp as he regularly walked about with a clip of money that contained hundreds of pounds, proudly getting out a fifty-pound note even to pay for the smallest of items.

My enduring memory of my father was his smell. As a confirmed pipe smoker, puffs of smoke signalled his arrival and on departure the aroma lingered with the memory of him. I still think of him whenever I am near a pipe smoker or smell the fragrance of that type of tobacco. It is one of those memories of the senses that I find hard to forget.

There was no Child Support Agency or legal enforcement for financial assistance from my father because I was illegitimate, and in those days that mattered. To all outward appearances he was jovial and generous, but in reality he was manipulative when it came to money and he only gave if he could get something in return. He didn't see child support as his responsibility and frequently tried to make my mother feel obliged to him if he gave her any money for my upkeep. Demanding that I be sent to him each weekend otherwise he would withhold payment, he was particularly difficult and spiteful if my mother asked for assistance in order to purchase clothing or any other necessities for me. Accusing her constantly of spending the money he gave to her on her other children, he was generous to a fault – and that fault was selfishness. For him, child support involved some kind of reciprocal arrangement and he simply couldn't understand that it was his duty as a father.

What he didn't realize was that I loved being with him and the promise of money was never my concern. I was too young to understand the maliciousness of his conduct, and that he should have provided for me regardless of time spent with him. I thought that he was fun, and the weekends I spent at his flat were a pleasure I looked forward to as his apartment was full of gadgets. He would let me stay up late to watch television, so in my eyes he was exciting and adventurous. Whilst there I was spoilt with gifts and attention, and I lapped it up as any child would, being completely oblivious of the spiteful behaviour he sometimes showed my mother. It was my belief that my father was the epitome of generosity.

From around the age of 7 I spent each Saturday afternoon at his barbershop. It was a hive of activity where men would gather and talk about cricket, music, local gossip and other topics I was too young to understand. Lively discussions on subjects such as the prowess of Viv Richards, the West Indian cricketer, would take place, and an outsider walking past would have been forgiven for thinking that an intense argument was in progress. The men jumping up and shouting at each other in disagreement always seemed to be on the verge of a fight, but never got that far. It was just the passionate, verbosity of middle-aged West Indian men.

I tried to be an able and attentive barbershop assistant, helping to sweep up, but most of the time I stood staring wide-eyed in fascination, playing with the soft brushes that my father used to disperse the hair that remained on his customers' necks. After they had finished, most of the patrons would give me ten pence, pat me on the head and express how like my father I was, and it made me proud to think that I looked like him. He was charming, and I had inherited his handsome smile and dimples. With the money I received I would buy sweets to share with my sisters when I got home, and I could get a lot for my money in those days. I felt rich in the love and attention I had from both my parents, but the idyll of my early years was something that I would forget as I got older.

When the Blossoms Changed

My father had many girlfriends, or 'Aunties' as I called them, and we would visit them after the shop had closed, when they too would spoil me with food, money and gifts. I think he knew that a cute child was an essential accessory for attracting women, and he had many ladies to impress, so I accompanied him everywhere. One of his ladies was called Aunty B. and I liked her most, which was fortunate as she soon became his exclusive girlfriend. She and her children would stop over at his apartment and the adults would have the main bedroom whilst her children and I shared the loft, which had two single beds in it. I was fascinated by them as they were from a country town and had strange accents, different to my inner-city Brummie tones.

One night after we had been sent to bed I was awakened by one of her older children who had a new game to play, which had to be played at night, and in bed. The teenager came into my bed and played the 'game', all the time saying that it was just a bit of fun. I was only little, but I instinctively knew that I didn't like the new game and it didn't seem like fun. Something inside me felt that it was wrong, and I couldn't understand why I disliked this person so much, even though they had previously been such a good playmate. Too young to understand what was happening I was sworn to secrecy, which wasn't hard, as at the time I really couldn't put into words what had occurred, but when I returned home after that particular visit to my father's, I changed.

First, I stuck by my mother like glue, and became her little shadow whenever she was around; I was very clingy, but couldn't and wouldn't say why. Then I became a nightmare to my siblings, showing off and parading my gifts to Special and Serene, as a result incurring their wrath, with bickering and fights taking place. I often wondered why I didn't tell, but I think it was because I didn't really understand the gravity of what had been done to me. As a result, it was not the only time such incidents occurred in my early childhood. Although there were times when I almost spoke to my mother about it, something inside always prevented me from doing so. I think it was the fear of the unknown. I was unsure of what was happening and so I remained silent. Yet the trauma of what I was enduring began to show, as I became reluctant to go to my father's, and cried, pleading with my mother to let me stay at home, though I couldn't tell her why. I became so distraught that the stay was cancelled and it was decided that I would just visit on the

Sunday instead. Even then I asked not to be sent on my own and fabricated a feeble excuse about being bored and lonely. I'm not sure whether my mother was truly convinced, but happily for me she complied and my sister Special became my companion to my father's for the next couple of Sundays. I was delighted that I didn't have to go alone and, most importantly, with Special in attendance I wouldn't be able to stay the night. I was overjoyed, but my father was not and he resented Special's company, showing his displeasure by sulking like a child. This continued for a few weekends but pretty soon he made his feelings known to my mother and I had to resume my weekend visits unaccompanied as before.

When he came to collect me and I discovered I had to stay overnight I felt anxious until I heard that we would be alone; Aunty B. and her family weren't going to be around any more. It was a relief, but I still felt uncomfortable at his flat and was quiet and moody despite his best efforts. Nothing he said or did made me feel better. Whereas before I would have run upstairs into his loft to create my own play, I was now scared of the shadows of what had occurred there. I couldn't be sure if he knew, as he seemed angry and began to drink. When he fell asleep in a drunken stupor I sat quietly, alternating between reading and watching him doze. I knew that he liked to drink, but never before had he been so intoxicated in my presence.

From then on he drank regularly, usually beginning with beer and then graduating to wine and eventually spirits. Each weekend I would become more reluctant to visit as I watched him graduate from happy social drinker to morose alcoholic. I would try to create an excuse not to go to my father's and sometimes it worked, but more often than not I had to attend.

View of Violence

One of the most memorable weekends I spent with my father began with our usual routine of my going to the shop with him and helping out. When we closed up and went back to his flat we counted the day's takings quietly but he didn't laugh and talk with me as he used to. I missed being able to rest my head on his soft, bulbous stomach whilst I listened to him tell Anansi Spider or Brer Rabbit stories. He had a deep bass voice, and when he spoke I could feel the vibrations of his words through his belly cushion. All these delights ceased as he drank and slept for hours.

When he finally woke up I asked if I could go home but my request was denied and instead he ordered me to get my coat on as we were going out. My heart sank when he said that we were going to see Aunty B. I wasn't sure what had happened but it seemed to be the cause of his foul mood. It was then I became fearful. Did he know? I didn't know whether the 'game' was right or wrong but I did know it made me feel bad so, thinking it might have been the cause of their break-up, I thought the best thing to do was say nothing and do as I was told.

It was getting dark by the time the taxi arrived. My father couldn't drive so we took taxis everywhere. The journey seemed to take forever and when we reached our destination it was pitch-dark and I was dreadfully afraid, still suffering my fear of the night. We were on streets that I didn't recognize and I later found out that we had driven all the way to the country town where Aunty B. lived, miles away from home. I had never been further than two miles away from home all my life. She lived in a terraced house with a tall, thin front door with peeling red paint that looked brown in the dark. My father rapped at it hard with his knuckles. When someone asked who it was, I knew it was Aunty B. and my father announced his name with purpose. I could hear her shuffle at the door but not open it, and an argument began, with both of them shouting. Screaming at her furiously to open up, my father's left hand was holding mine tightly whilst his other was in a fist pounding the door. With each pound my wrist ached as he jerked my body as though I were a bag he was holding and not his daughter. The noise they were making made their words unintelligible and at 8 years old I didn't understand a thing being said, but Aunty B. must have wanted to avoid a scene because eventually, albeit reluctantly, she opened the door. Holding it slightly ajar and barely showing her face through it, she tried to reason with him, but as she did he pushed the door wide open.

In a split second there was a slamming noise that could have been mistaken for the door ricocheting off its hinges, but it wasn't. The solid cracking sound was his hand making contact with her face as he struck her with his fist. The hand that had been holding mine released me from its grasp and with both hands he battered her with such force that blood began to pour from her mouth. I froze as I watched him beat her. The whole scene played out like images on a filmstrip and, frame by frame, motion by motion, my eyes and mind viewed and absorbed the violence. The only movement I made was when I shivered as she let out a final scream and her body hit the ground.

Lights came on upstairs and before anyone else could intervene he grabbed my arm and dragged me to the waiting taxi, moving so fast I thought my limb was going to be pulled out of its socket as I struggled to keep up with him. As soon as we were seated I threw up and the taxi driver complained, but quickly quietened down when my father waved a full clip of money at him, promising adequate compensation as long as he drove us back to Birmingham. As we started on our way he looked at me, grabbed my arm again and pulled me close. He spoke to me as never before, in a cutting tone, the memory of which still sends chills down my spine, 'Don't you tell your mother. Keep your big mouth shut. D'you hear me?'

I tried to say, 'Yes Daddy', but all I could do was nod in acknowledgement. I was dumbstruck. I had never seen such violence before, not even on television; I wasn't allowed. I wondered if she was dead, as when we left she wasn't moving. I hadn't seen a dead body, apart from those in the murder mysteries on television, and it didn't look like a movie to me. Had he killed her? Would he beat me if I told? Would he beat Mom? I couldn't hold back the gagging feeling in my throat and I shook with fear, closing my eyes, too afraid to open them and look at him. I couldn't stop crying even though he kept telling me to stop. Everything changed; from that moment on he was unrecognizable as my daddy. It was as though he no longer saw me as a child, and I knew I would never be able to hug and hold him as I had before.

When we arrived back in Birmingham, instead of going to his flat he took me home. Holding my hand tightly as he handed me to my mother he lied to her, saying that he'd decided to bring me home because I was ill. From the way he squeezed my hand when he said it I knew that he was reiterating to me the necessity of silence. I knew he was lying, but she had no reason to believe otherwise, and I was immediately taken upstairs where I promptly threw up again. He said nothing as he left but glanced up the stairs and gave me a look that spoke volumes.

Within hours I was taken to hospital as I kept being sick, but upon examination they could find nothing wrong, and my mother was told that I probably had a stomach bug and that I was to rest. I knew differently. Sheer terror was making me sick and fear increased its hold on me as I thought of the consequences of telling my mother. I believed he would hit or kill her, and I wasn't even sure if Aunty B. was alive or dead. It was the biggest secret I'd ever had to keep, and for the first time in my life I was afraid of my father. It was impossible to tell my mother because I believed I had to keep her safe. Every time I closed my eyes I could see what happened, and it made me vomit. I therefore stayed in bed not eating or drinking, determined not to break the silence.

It was late Sunday evening when my mother received a phone call. She was downstairs in the living room and from my bed upstairs I could hear her. She didn't seem to be doing much talking, just listening and saying, 'Mmm hmm' a lot, but within minutes she put down the phone and ran upstairs. Panic stricken, thoughts assailed my mind. Was it Dad on the phone? Did he think that I had told? The more I thought of him, more sickness rose in my throat, and when she came into the room and sat on the bed I wrapped my arms around her waist tightly, hoping that he hadn't called and that he wasn't going to kill her too.

'Claudette, what is it? Did something happen yesterday? Did something happen with Daddy and Aunty B.?' She spoke in such a way as to try to get me to tell the secret that she now knew I was keeping.

I could hear my heart beat so loudly that I thought it was about to burst open, and before I knew it I burst into tears, yet I still couldn't tell. Fear gripped my mind and I knew that my father would be mad, and I had to protect my mother from such violence. I felt the burden of a secret untold, although I wanted to have it taken from me. Not knowing what to do or say, all I could do was cry.

'That was Aunty B. on the phone,' she said. 'She rang to see if you were alright after what happened. She told me everything. It's alright, I know.'

'You know?' I whispered. My eyes popped wide open and I stopped crying.

'Yes, I know.'

Oh, the relief I felt as I looked up at her face, knowing that Aunty B. was alive. I also saw that my mother knew and nothing untoward had happened to her, and with those words I was free from the awful secret. Aunty B. had called my mother to see how I was after what I had witnessed, and when I knew that she wasn't dead I immediately sat up, hugged my mother and cried, but this time from relief. Wanting to hear from me everything that happened I told her everything I saw, and she chastised me, saying that I could always tell her anything. I was sorry and explained how I had been sworn to secrecy, and was still scared but also relieved that I hadn't told.

Within minutes I no longer felt sick, but was hungry. After some toast and tea, I was up and playing in no time. My mother had the inevitable 'words' with my father and I didn't then see him for quite a few weeks, which wasn't unusual. Whenever he fell out with her he would mope and stay away, before finally cooling off and turning up to apologize – and in time he came over to apologize to me. Well, he never actually said sorry or talked about the incident, but he said it in his own way with gifts galore. Naturally, as a child, I forgave him – but though forgiven, the incident was never forgotten.

This was the beginning of my 'spring' and seeds of abuse, buds of mistrust and fear were the blossoms of the season. The season's 'must-have' outfits were silence and secrecy, but although these two garments were ill-fitting and did not suit me well, I learned that I had to wear them in order to survive. In fact, I found the only way I could carry the silence of abuse and what I had witnessed my father do was to block them out of my mind. I really didn't think about them again, as I knew that if I did I would end up being sick. As I look back I can now can see how an 8-year-old child who was adored and loved by her family started to feel unloved. It was an awakening that I shouldn't have experienced, yet at the time I thought that this was normal life. I thought everyone had a childhood like mine and knew no different. To me, my father's way was the way of all fathers – I didn't know any better since he was the only father I had. At such a young age I didn't understand any of it, yet it had happened; I could not turn back time and I was going to have to live with it.

3
It's Getting Cold Out There . . .

Even a child is known by his deeds, whether what he does is pure and right.
Proverbs 20:11 (NKJV)

Before the spring awakenings I'd had a blissful infanthood at school and home. It was bright and happy, and I had plenty of friends. I remember playing outside, lots of laughter and songs, and being the blithe Sunday's child without a care in the world. Sadly, I also remember when it all changed. My sisters Special and Serene moved on to senior school, and the older children in the family were at college or work, and for the first time I was going to be at school with no relatives present. It didn't bother me as I was looking forward to embarking on a new era of independence. My only concern was that I would not have their company when I walked home from school, but as we only lived a short distance away I dismissed that worry quickly enough. I was relatively happy, all things considered, although I had changed somewhat due to what had happened at my father's. Essentially, however, I remained the same smiley child I had always been.

For four years I'd had the friendships of Lady, a pretty and amusing black girl, and Sai, a happy-go-lucky white girl. We had started primary school together, and at nearly 9 years old it seemed that our friendship would last forever. Despite returning to school after the six-week holiday to find new people in attendance, I naturally assumed my childhood friends and I would stick together. I did my best to integrate with the new children that were in our classroom, but there was one particular girl that I just couldn't gel with. The girl concerned was tall, slim and black, and her clothes were scruffy and had seen better days. Her skin was rough and dry and looked as though it needed a good creaming. In those days we didn't have to wear school uniforms and it was obvious who came from the poorer families or were neglected. My family weren't wealthy by any means, but no matter how financially strapped our mother was she never let us out of the house in a rumpled state. Clothes displayed status and hair, which we black girls wore in plaits or cornrows, was regularly renewed with precision and care by our mothers, who took pride in our appearances – that is, all except for 'New Girl'. Of course, New Girl was not her name, but it sums up how I remember her. In my memory she was an entity and not a being, a person without personality, a girl who should have mattered little to me – but she became the most important thing in my life from the first day I met her.

I must have appeared to be the very opposite to New Girl, as my hair was dressed in ribbons by Pearl and although I wore hand-me-downs they were well-kept, washed and ironed. I was in the top sets of my classes and was an avid reader, and when New Girl spoke it seemed to me that she was not very bright. I discussed this amongst my friends as we got to know the new people in our class. She struggled academically and the Janet and John children's books that we were reading were too difficult for her. It became obvious pretty quickly that we did not like each other, and although I befriended her initially, inviting her into my circle of friends, I watched her with suspicion.

My life at school changed from that term. First there were childish squabbles and jealousies that I took part in, sometimes trying to be the peacemaker but more often than not ending up the troublemaker. Then children told lies, as children do, and friends broke up and made up, time and again. This cycle continued for a while and seemed to consist of harmless childhood spats, easily resolved with a quick 'Sorry' and 'Let's make friends', but somehow it escalated. Most of the arguments revolved around New Girl, yet whenever our paths crossed it always got personal and she would fall out with me longer than with my other friends. She'd call me fat or the teacher's pet and said that I thought I was posh. Although I took it on the chin, when it came to making friends again New Girl didn't want to and eventually, one by one, my friends were taken away. In a few short weeks the girls that had been my friends became exclusively New Girl's friends and, thereafter, my enemies.

Looking back I believe that New Girl prevailed in the friendship stakes because my personality had changed. Because of what I had seen and experienced I had become less friendly and was suspicious of new people. The buds of mistrust were starting to bloom, and in the end I had so many fall-outs that no one was speaking to me. Ostracized by my peers, I resorted to playing with the younger children at playtimes and hoped that one day I would be accepted back into the circle of friends I had grown up with.

Toughening Up

About halfway through the term, one break time, some of the girls that had stopped speaking to me asked me to play. I was happy that I was going to be friends with them again; it was all I wanted. I had even hoped to make up with New Girl, and as we walked to the netball court I apologized and made friends again with Lady and Sai, and they led me to believe that reconciliation with New Girl was imminent. The netball court was really just a concrete playground with rudimentary markings and as I got there I saw New Girl with some other girls. I smiled at her but she didn't respond. She didn't seem to mind that I was going to play, though, and we stood on the court together, ten girls in all, including me. The game started and they passed the ball to each other, and I stood by waiting for someone on my team to pass it to me. I was open and clearly able to take the ball, and I called out to my old friend Lady, but she ignored me even though she had picked me for her team. Throwing the ball between each other, back and forth, and bypassing me each time, the girls continued to play. I was confused as I stood there on the court while they passed the ball around me, playing with each other. I called out again, in the hope that they would let me join in, and then it happened; the trick was played. In one fell swoop they gathered around me in a circle.

'What are you doing here? Who asked you to play, you fat, ugly b****?' New Girl shouted in my face. She pushed my shoulder and spat on me. That was just the beginning, for soon they all joined in, pushing and kicking at my legs. The horror that I felt was visible on my face, as it dawned on me why they had asked me to play. I had been set up. They had asked me to play in order to beat me up. That was my first experience of bullying and it was to affect my ability to trust others for the rest of my life.

When my mother got in from work that evening I told her about what had happened. As I had been having difficulties with the girls for some time, I think she thought that the conflict was in the same category and, to be honest, so did I. I never thought that day would be repeated. She assured me that the next day it would be OK. She called the school to complain about it, although we believed that it was a one-off incident. In retrospect I can understand why we thought that, as now that I'm a mother myself I've seen my children fall out with their friends and make up just as easily. We thought that it was just one of those situations. I took my mother's advice and hoped that the situation would blow over and everything would go back to normal.

The next day, however, I had to get used to a new kind of 'normal'. Each break time I was taunted and teased and it continued the next day, and every day after that. I was pushed around the playground and frogmarched into a corner, where they surrounded me and called me derogatory names. The girls were clever about not being caught. It was common during break times for children to give performances of songs to which others would be the audience. Whenever a teacher got near, they would quickly change from bullying me to pretending to be a crowd watching a song and dance. As soon as the teacher was gone they would taunt me again, and it was relentless. There was little adult supervision. I was an easy target. The names usually had something to do with my weight – I was fat; or my skin – I was too dark or it was blotchy; or my hair – it was rubbish. My whole appearance was torn apart and when they got tired of that a new approach was taken. They picked on my intelligence and teased the fact that I liked to answer questions that the teacher put to the class. Sneered and jeered at, both in and out of the classroom, I retreated into myself and stopped participating in class for fear of being singled out. The end of each day contained a threat that if I told anyone I'd get beaten up and I was threatened with the brute force of their older brothers. Terrified, I obliged and kept quiet or played down the extent of the bullying to my mother.

When I got home I'd tell her some of what was happening and she tried to give me tactics for combating the bullies. I received lots of advice and strategies. When they whispered threats in the classroom, I shouted back telling them to leave me alone. But that only resulted in ridicule. I told the teacher, and that was one of the biggest mistakes I made, because after I did I was ostracized by the whole class. Each strategy I tried failed miserably to the point that

I kept the bullying to myself, for fear of repercussions. Nevertheless, after a whole term of teasing and bullying I finally told my mother that it was getting worse and she made an appointment with the headmaster to discuss the matter. At the meeting he assured her that he had it in hand and that he would deal with it.

The next day when I went into school I nervously waited all day, wondering what the headmaster would do about the bullies. I thought nothing had been done, until late in the afternoon just before school ended I was called out of class into his office. To my surprise the bullies were there as well. Astonishingly, the man felt that the best way to resolve the situation was to stand me in front of New Girl and two of the other bullies. Then he asked me what they were doing to me. He was a large, imposing man and he towered over me in interrogation, but the fear I felt for him was nothing compared to my fear of the girls. He wanted me to speak in the presence of the very girls that were bullying me. It was ridiculous to say the least, as I knew that if I snitched I would suffer even more the next day. New Girl gave me a look that told me to keep my mouth shut; I knew exactly what it meant as I had seen the same look from my father. In fear I played down the true extent of the bullying and once again it was looked upon as a childhood spat. We were made to shake hands and say sorry to each other as if we'd had a minor fall-out. When I look back I can see that it was handled very badly, as the headmaster's actions ensured I was in for it in a big way.

As predicted, the bullying got worse: even though I hadn't told the truth about them, the fact that the headmaster had been involved was enough. The bullies wanted to exact some kind of revenge. The headmaster had asked the dinner ladies to watch out for me in the playground, so I stood close to them, hoping that if I stood next to an adult the bullies couldn't get me, but I was wrong. The bullies followed me home after school each night, and I was pushed and prodded all the way to the bottom of my road. The names I was called were vile and soul-destroying; it hadn't stopped and was getting worse.

In class, the other children were ordered by New Girl not to have anything to do with me and so the isolation began. No one wanted to sit next to me, or work with me, and I never had a partner for any activities. Sport was the worst since I was never picked for a team and was ridiculed, ignored and derided during each game. When the teachers observed what was happening they felt that the best course of action would be to move me up into the next year group, as I was bright enough to cope with the work and it would separate me from the gang that so obviously hated me. It was a short-sighted solution to a long-term problem as, although I was away from the bullies in the classroom, whenever the dinner ladies weren't there I still had to face them – at break times and on the way home. Soon the school decided I should spend lunchtimes in the classroom with my teacher, but this only served to isolate me from the other children and confirmed the title of Teacher's Pet. I was completely alone. The children in my year group didn't play with me, as they were older than me, and in my own class no one spoke to me. I even tried to make friends with younger children, but the bullies would threaten them with the same treatment they had seen me receive.

The avoidance tactics the school employed only worked sporadically. There was no guarantee that the dinner ladies would look after me and my class teacher was soon fed up of not being able to go to lunch with the other staff, so I had to go out to play again. Before long the torment intensified as I was pushed around the playground each break and followed home at the end of every school day. Sometimes it was the whole gang of nine, or sometimes just a couple of girls, some of whom had once been my friends. When they used profanities and called me names, I believed the things they said about me. Even other children that I didn't know would call me names such as 'Fatty-bum bum', and I became an available target for all. I was slowly tormented, with my self-esteem being stripped away with every caustic jibe. It continued for the rest of the year at school, and fear consumed me. I was so scared of the bullies that their power over me was real and it made me too afraid to tell anyone how bad it was getting. This, coupled with the school's refusal to acknowledge the girls' behaviour as bullying and insistence that it was just childhood arguments, contributed to my belief that I was too soft or too sensitive – I believed I was weak.

I remember one day when we had a school trip to a city farm. I foolishly asked a question about a very large brown horse that was being groomed. New Girl sniggered as I asked about the horse's name and 'Bouncer' was the response. It was a question that I regretted asking, as from that day on I was called by that name. No one called me

Claudette any more; instead I was Bouncer, the girl as fat as the horse, with hair like the horse, as ugly as the horse and as smelly as a horse. I remember this vividly and the emotions I felt are with me as I write. It is heartbreaking to recall those years; the memories of their cruelty still make me cry.

I tried everything I could to win my friends back and began using any tuck money that my mother gave me to buy sweets to gain their favour. It worked only in the moment; they would be nice when I had sweets, but as soon as they were gone they turned on me once more. So I started stealing in order to buy more and ended up stealing from my mother's purse, and surreptitiously taking any spare change I could find around the house to buy sweets. This was all in an effort to get them to like me. My mother accused one of my brothers of stealing and I never confessed. I was too scared, so I let others take the blame. I also stole at school and hung around the cloakroom going through people's pockets to see what I could find. The cloakroom was also a good hiding place away from the bullies.

Just before the summer break there came another incident that further singled me out from other children. I was sitting in class and had severe stomach ache all day. I endured it until close to the end of the day when I asked the teacher if I could go home. To my surprise she agreed, and for the first time in months I was not followed home. When I got in I ran upstairs and sat in the bathroom stubbornly refusing to move until my mother came home. I waited for more than two hours, locking myself in, and one by one family members came home and shouted through the bathroom door, trying to help me. I refused, as something had happened that I didn't want anyone to see. When my mother came home she ran upstairs and ordered me to open the door. I did, and with the worries of the world on my shoulders I told her the awful truth. I was dying. My life was over. But instead of the sympathy that I expected, my mother breathed a huge sigh of relief and laughed. To say I was confused would be an understatement. Why was she laughing when I was obviously dying?

'Serene, go and get some of those things that ladies use,' she shouted through the open door whilst shaking her head and laughing.

It was only when she explained what it was that I understood her laughter. She was relieved that it was nothing more serious than the stuff of life and womanhood. I was 9 years old and had no idea about the facts of life, but that day I was given the talk about the birds and the bees. She was amazed I had developed so early and realized that the issue of my puppy fat had in fact been the first buds of a figure. Smiling and comforting her baby, she told me that it was something special and meant that I was growing up. For me, it felt that once again I had something that made me the odd one out at school.

Living for the Weekend

Although school was a living nightmare, I had a respite from my troubles at weekends and I loved it when they came. We followed the Saturday routine and as music flowed through the house I was able to forget about the bullying. When my sisters and I pretended to be Sister Sledge, and choreographed dances and sang, I was happy. Sundays were bittersweet, with a visit to church and my father's. Things had changed with my father but not church. For years I had heard about the Bible, learning from the Old and New Testament, completing quizzes and learning Scripture verses by heart. Each week I was desperate to get to my Sunday school teacher so I could tell her the verse I had memorized and get my sticker. I had received many books at Sunday school but still awaited the coveted prize of a new Good News Children's Bible, fully illustrated. I had seen one that others had won, and I was determined to get mine, as it was beautiful. I wasn't sure I would if they found out I'd been stealing, however, so I tried to forget about the bullies and my own misdemeanours and just live for the weekend.

I was Sunday's child again, bonny and happy. It was the only time when I was with other children that I felt as though I belonged. Church gave us all something in common and that was what I wanted, and I didn't have to worry about making friends whilst there as there simply wasn't time. It was a place of retreat, a place to learn and think of better things and a better tomorrow. It was my Sunday piece of heaven before the 'hell' of the week at school. We sang such songs of joy and learned about people in the Bible who had overcome terrible adversities. In each story God sent a miracle and I wanted my own, and I prayed each night that it would come. All I wanted was a friend, but it seemed it wasn't to be. I had been attending the Sunday school since the age of 5 and it came to mean more to me than ever before because it gave me the strength I needed to face the week ahead. In my mind, whilst I was at church or at home, school did not exist.

It was only on Monday morning that I woke to the reality of being a perpetual victim. As lovely as Sundays were, I went to bed each Sunday night mentally preparing for what I would have to face, and the only way I could do that was to try not to think of it. I prayed for God to help me and not let them bully me, but Monday would bring its trouble, week in and week out. It was relentless.

Although the following summer holiday brought a break from it all, the bubbly, spoilt, youngest child that I had been had turned into an introverted, shy recluse. I resorted to wearing a big woolly hat at all times to cover my hair, as the girls had said it was horrible and I believed them. I occupied my time during the summer by reading and playing with dolls, and I completely blocked out any thoughts of school. Although I dreaded returning there after the summer, I chose not to think about it, and if by chance I did I would freeze and mentally block out the feelings of fear that threatened to invade my being. It became my coping strategy.

In my final year of junior school I was once again in the same class as the bullies. The year before my mother had visited the headmaster numerous times in an effort to get him to deal with them. This had not been forgotten and the girls were eager to get revenge. So I endured another year of bullying. The name calling was now standard. I believed that I was ugly, inside and out, and that it must have been my fault – that they hated me because of something to do with my personality. For two years, every school morning, fear and anxiety woke me up, nausea breakfasted with me, and terror walked me to school. I'd pray that I would just be left alone, just for once, and sometimes I was, but it was very rare.

When I say to people that I had no friends I'm sure they think that I am exaggerating, but I'm not. I didn't play with the other children in school and, if I couldn't hide next to a dinner lady at playtime, I would try to hide in a corner where no one could see me. My only safe havens were church and home, and even then I had the issue of an alcoholic father to contend with. My childhood was stripped from me each day I was there. Daily I wished my sisters were with me, as when they had been there no one bothered me. I felt alone, with no one to talk to or help me. When we talk about it now my mother says that I never really told her how bad it was, and perhaps she is right. I thought I did, but I foolishly believed that I was weaker than my sisters for allowing myself to be bullied. It was hard to stand up for myself when it was just not in my nature. In family discussions I was told I was too sensitive, which made me think that being sensitive was a bad thing. It was only words, and I shouldn't have let them affect me – but they did and I couldn't tell anyone how badly it hurt. It seemed as though it was my fault that I couldn't take the verbal abuse. It was my fault that they picked on me: I wasn't friendly or I was just – yes, again – too sensitive. I began to hate the word. Being sensitive epitomized weakness and vulnerability, and I believed I should not be vulnerable. I had to learn to block things out, and so frost appeared in my heart. I could feel it destroying the initial blossoms of faith, joy and love I had once cherished.

It was spring and weeds were growing. The harsh frost of isolation that came at such a delicate time of my life proved too much for the tender root of happiness that I had left after the abuse. It was vulnerable, and exposure to dramatic changes in conditions proved detrimental. So I decided that I wouldn't feel anything any more, and the only way to do that was to establish a routine of wiping the day from my memory. As soon as I got home from school I didn't think about it and I lived in a fantasy world. I listened to music, watched television, or read a book – anything to block out the day. Daydreaming became a constant pastime and as long as I was someone else, anyone else but me, I somehow managed to survive.

4
Colder and Tougher Still

Do not seek revenge or bear a grudge against anyone among your people, but love your neighbour as yourself . . .

Leviticus 19:18

My childhood was not all doom and gloom, as I did have happy times at home. I felt happiest when I was around my big brother, Art, who had a moped and then a motorbike on which secretly he took my sisters and me for rides. Our mother did not approve. I didn't confide in Art, but when I was with him I didn't think about the bullies. I'd help him with any work he brought home, sitting indoors with my big woolly hat on and chatting away to my big brother who indulged me. He was a keen cook and together we'd try new recipes we'd found and then add a Caribbean twist to them. He taught me to experiment with cooking and quietly we'd create our concoctions and feed the family with new and exciting meals. When I wasn't at my father's for the weekend I'd bother Art, and if I wasn't with him, I'd go into my world of fantasy and stay there for the duration of the weekend.

My eldest brother Indie was an infrequent visitor to the house and by the time I was 11 years old he was a father too. A heavy goods vehicle driver by trade, he had a fancy car, and Art was soon to follow and buy a car himself. It was Indie's car that was the most memorable, however – not that I remember the make of vehicle or colour, but what I do remember is that our mother strictly forbade him from taking us for a drive. He was a hotshot driver and she believed he drove too fast and too erratically, but like most children we begged our big brother to take us for a drive and, unable to resist the temptation to show his skills, Indie obliged. Needless to say, the escapade resulted in my first ever car crash, and that was the memorable thing, for it was one more incident that involved me being sworn to secrecy. It wasn't a problem, as I had learned the necessity of keeping quiet about things. Nevertheless, our mother did find out and Indie was verbally chastised, only to turn up a few weeks later with his lorry from work. There was *no way* I was going to miss a ride in that, so all the kids hopped aboard the gargantuan truck. I was lifted into the huge cabin and sat next to the oversized steering wheel. That drive and that day was one of the best days of my childhood. We only went for a short ride but I will never forget how special it felt, riding in my big brother's lorry, and I remember wishing that all my days could be like that.

In retrospect I see that my two eldest brothers were like the father that I wished I had. I never had to endure afternoons of drunkenness with them and, unbeknown to them, they were my father figures, especially Art. My young life was a mixture of these days of youthful happiness juxtaposed with weekly experiences of mental torture, and I became two people – the happy child at home and the quiet bullied child at school.

Towards the end of the two years the gang bullied me more out of routine and habit, as the malicious intent abated and a 'normality' set in with regards to their behaviour towards me. But it was still hard. I got used to being the victim but I hated it, and I believed I had to take matters into my own hands. My prayers had apparently not been listened to because they hadn't been answered. I had asked for a friend, but I had none. I had learned about a better tomorrow, but none had come, so I decided to make it better for myself. Things were changing, and I was even growing apart from my sisters as they turned into teenagers and I became the annoying little sister. After two years of being called Bouncer and Fatty, and of being afraid to go out and play, something had to give. I'd had enough. The victim had to disappear and I had to get tough, strong and hard. I made up my mind that I wouldn't let them hurt me again.

One week I followed my usual routine of finding hiding places and trying to avoid bullies, but while I did I began to despise the fact that I was hiding, cowering in weakness. By Friday my mind was made up that I had to do something, but I didn't know what. As I walked back into school after the lunch break, I was relieved that I hadn't had to deal with them that day, not just out of fear, but because I wasn't sure what I would do. I reached the bottom of the stairway that led to the entrance and took an anxious deep breath as I saw a group of children on a balcony that led to the foyer. My fear left when I saw it wasn't the bullies and, relieved, I made my way into school, but therein lay my error, for as I turned the corner to walk through the main door the girls were waiting for me.

New Girl came strutting towards me, with all the swagger of a girl spoiling for a fight. With her face so close to mine that I could smell her breath as she talked, she laughed as the other girls surrounded me. She and I were encircled by eight girls and I closed my eyes, waiting for her to reel off the same abusive diatribe I had heard for two exhausting years. She didn't disappoint, but then for some reason brought up the arguments we'd had at the beginning of her time at school. Lady, who had previously been my friend, told her that I had said she was a tramp, and she latched on to that as if I had been taunting her with it for two years instead of her bullying me. With indignation she shouted at me for calling her a name and used the power it gave her to become even viler than I thought she could be. She cursed me repeatedly and I shook, and she must have thought that it was a sign of fear for she raised her hand and slapped my face. It stung my cheek and for the first time in my life I swore, but instead of freezing with fear as usual, a strange feeling I had never felt before came over me. It grew and spread down my arms like the blood that pulsed through my veins and before I knew what I was doing my hand was in a fist and I struck her hard on her cheek.

She stumbled backwards and looked stunned. She had not been prepared for me to fight back as I had never done so before, but something had changed. Frost had taken hold of my heart and it had turned it cold with bitterness and hate. It was that day that I knew what it was to truly hate someone and I hated her, I hated all of them and I told her so.

'I hate you. You *are* a tramp, a dutty [dirty] tramp,' I said as I took joy in watching the shock on her face that I dared to speak back to her.

Before I knew it fists were flying, but they were not hers – they were mine. I don't think she knew what hit her as I pummelled her stomach and purposefully landed blow after blow, just as I had seen my father do to Aunty B. It was the first time in my life that I had really fought back, and the first time I felt such rage. As I did, I beat everyone that had ever hurt me. She tried to fight and kick at me, but I knew I could take her. I knew that if I had enough hate I would have the strength to defeat her and be just like my father. She and her gang of bullies had shown me nothing but hatred, so I was now going to take revenge and I fought with all my might.

Sadly, my rage was not enough for me to be able to fight all the bullies at once, because soon they all joined in. My clothes were ripped, my hair pulled out, they scratched my face and neck, and kicked my legs and stomach. It was brutal. The fight only lasted a few minutes, but it felt as though time had stopped whilst I was repeatedly kicked and beaten by all nine girls. A large crowd gathered around, which drew the attention of the teachers who dispersed the crowd and pulled the girls off me. With blood pouring from my neck, and my arms and legs scratched, I cried. I didn't cry because of the pain; I cried because I had acted like my father.

I honestly thought that I would feel better after I had retaliated, but I didn't. I thought I would feel victorious, vindicated, free and, most of all, powerful. Vengeance would somehow pay for the pain they had caused me. All the lessons that I had learned in Sunday school told me that fighting wasn't right, however. I was taught to love and forgive but I couldn't. I wanted to do things the Christian way by turning the other cheek, and I had even tried it, but I didn't think it worked so I took the matter into my own hands. But the end result wasn't what I'd hoped for. Yes, I'd shown them I was no longer a victim, but I couldn't shake the feeling that I had lowered myself and become just like them and, worse still, like my father. In a rage of hate I had thrown aside my faith, but the inner pain I felt was worse than what the bullies had done to me. I didn't like the hate I felt, and I certainly didn't like to fight, but it was all I could do; I felt I was fighting the battle on my own. Once again, the school dealt with it in their own unique way. Instead of disciplining the girls, they sent me home after being told that I had struck the first blow. There was nothing I could say, it was their word against mine and I had no one on my side as a witness, even though it was nine girls against one.

Face to Face

I didn't know that day would be so significant. When my mother came home and saw what they had done she declared she'd had enough. She had tried to deal with it through the school to no avail; their methods were obviously not working and now it was her turn. In those days, as a single black mother dealing with a predominantly white education system, she must have felt she had to follow the guidance given by the establishment, but she knew it had to be done the West Indian way, which is face to face. It can be confrontational, but it was the only way and my mother knew it.

My mother is a quiet woman, a true Bajan beauty both in looks and conduct, by which I mean she displays the elegance and gentility of times long gone. She is not given to outbursts of extreme emotions, happy or sad. When her temper was roused, therefore, it was a sight to behold, and we all stood out of the way when she was angry. When this happened, she was livid. She was going to deal with it herself, once and for all. Not being able to drive, she called Indie and asked him to take us to each girl's house. I knew where most of them lived, as they had previously been my friends, and I was made to point out their homes as we drove around. I didn't really want to, as I was scared of what would happen, but my mother looked so determined that I knew I had to comply. My brother Troy came along as well and with him being more than six foot tall it was like coming with the heavy mob. My big brothers and my mother were dealing with something I wished had been dealt with a long time before. It took the whole evening, and she went to each house and spoke to every parent, showing them the state of me and explaining what their child had done, and had been doing to me for the past two years. She was eerily calm and polite, and it was very unnerving. Ladylike even when angry, she demanded an apology from each child and after she had finished speaking to them their parents apologized also. With my two brothers standing either side of her, she made the bullies and their parents aware that I wasn't alone and that I had a large family they would have to contend with if the bullying continued.

The last house we went to was New Girl's. When we got there I was not surprised at the state she lived in, but I was surprised at the similarities between us. She lived in a council house just like me, we both came from single-parent families and were children of first-generation Caribbean immigrants. We should have been allies. But the similarities stopped there. Her house was unkempt, and in comparison the home our mother kept seemed like Buckingham Palace. At school her clothes were always dirty but I was dressed immaculately, as even without a washing machine my mother scrubbed our clothes in the bath until they squeaked their cleanliness and begged for mercy.

I realized that we girls were the same person, two sides of the same coin, but I was the other 'her', living a parallel life but with a distinct difference. I had a mother that cared for me, and she had one that looked as though she was trying to come off the latest drug of choice. She didn't seem to care about her child and I got the feeling that, if the shoe were on other foot, New Girl's mother wouldn't spend a whole evening confronting her child's bullies and their parents. As my mother gave a stern talking to New Girl's mother, I smirked and felt no charity as the bully stood quietly. Her mother then pinched her arm and I saw fear in her eyes. I now wonder about that. Just as I had learned my rage from my father maybe she had learned her bullying ways from her mother, because New Girl squirmed and looked terrified.

She looked very much the little 11-year-old girl that she was and not the figure of the big bully. I took pleasure in the look of fear I saw in her eyes and I gave her a look as if to say, 'One day, when you are on your own, I am going to get you.' I held back my tears as my mother gave a strong ultimatum about the cessation of the bullying. With two of my brothers standing beside her it was an imposing statement of solidarity. My family weren't perfect, but they were there for me and perhaps if I had told my mother from the beginning how bad it was it would have been dealt with earlier.

That day I learned, though, that revenge hurts the avenger because it covered me in the cold, bitter coat of hate. It was a garment that squeezed and choked me tightly, restricting the love that I really wanted and needed. Vengeance was cold and brought no comfort, and when I got home I couldn't help but cry. I cried because deep down I knew it was not how I wanted to feel. I didn't regret standing up for myself, but the hatred I felt bothered me.

In that one evening two years of bullying ended. My mother was my hero and came to the rescue, but sadly the damage had already been done. I believed that the way I looked was the reason why everyone hated me. I was fat. I had been taunted so many times by the gang saying that I was fat and ugly that I believed them, and from then on no one and nothing could convince me that I was beautiful. New Girl had chosen that day to attack as it was the last day of that half term. She thought she could give me a beating and send me on my way in fear of her, but although I fought back and had a kind of victory I still worried about what the future held.

I was now on half-term break and my mother had dealt with the bullies but over the week I became anxious that things would get worse when I returned to school for the final few weeks.

After Art had taught me to experiment with recipes, I began to cook for myself and the family, not the traditional food of my culture but new, unusual 'foreign' foods such as pasta, lasagne and Chinese (well, they are foreign foods for a Caribbean household living in England). Whenever the family wanted a different meal cooked I would volunteer, but sometimes I would cook excess quantities of food and eat it all secretly. That half-term holiday, in the daytime whilst most of the family were at work or in their rooms, I'd prepare the evening meal but make sure I cooked extra so that I could comfort myself with food. One day I did and felt so sick afterwards that I put my fingers down my throat and brought it back up. I couldn't understand why it felt good to have overeaten and then cleansed myself from it, but I knew that I liked it. It was the beginning of a new relationship for me. I was just 11 years old and had begun a love–hate affair with the mental torment that is Bulimia.

The After-Effects of Spring

The after-effects of spring were that there were no pretty blossoms flourishing in my heart and I had an eating disorder, although I didn't know it at the time. The frost of hate had destroyed any growth of love, trust and friendship I may have had, and those years did more damage to my self-esteem than any of the events that followed. I was on my way to becoming unloved, yet when I look back I can see how much love there was surrounding me as my family came to the rescue. I also had the love of church, as it was still my Sunday piece of heaven – that was, until I fought back. When hate prevailed as a dominant emotion I wasn't sure what to feel any more and as a result was despondent. I'd heard stories of Jesus and how he loved people, and had marvelled at how he would talk to the unwanted, despised and disregarded. He seemed to love the unlovable and I wanted to do what he did but found it impossible to love the bullies. I didn't believe God was listening to me, as I had asked him for help repeatedly but the bullying hadn't stopped. I believed there was a God, and I believed he was there – but I wasn't sure if he was there for me.

One day during that half-term break I sat at the foot of my bed. Tears were rolling down my face onto my lips and the taste of their saltiness made me feel nauseous. I didn't moan or cry out but quietly caught each drop on my upper lip and licked them with my tongue, trying to increase the feeling of nausea, hoping that maybe I'd feel better again if I made myself sick. When my nose started to run I got up to get a tissue to wipe it. As I did, I stopped myself and said aloud, 'What's the point? It would be better to die than face school again.'

Those words sparked a chain of thoughts in my imma-ture spiritual mind. If I died, perhaps I would get that 'bet-ter tomorrow' they talked about in Sunday school? I would go to heaven and be free from the worry, the bullies, my father and any other 'aunties' and their children. At the grand old age of 11, I contemplated suicide and soon decided that it was my only option. Having seen it in movies, I thought I knew what to do. A peculiar sense of completion came over me as I went downstairs with tears still pouring down my face. It was as though I was floating, as I watched myself walk into the kitchen and open a drawer in order to find a knife.

'It would be easy. It would all be over, and I would never have to face school again,' I told myself repeatedly in order to cement my decision to take my life.

Picking up the sharpest knife I could find, a serrated blade with a brown wooden handle, I floated back upstairs with it in my hand. I imagined cutting my wrists and then closing my eyes to sleep forever. I daydreamed about how peaceful it would be compared to going back to school. I couldn't go back, I didn't want to – and I didn't want to live.

A voice jolted me back into reality.

'Claudette, where are you going with that knife?'

It was my brother Troy and he had caught sight of me as I walked up the stairs.

In an instant, the gravity of what I was about to do hit me. I made some kind of feeble excuse about cutting an apple and quickly ran back downstairs, putting the knife away. With it I put away the suicidal trance to which I had succumbed. My brother didn't know that he had saved my life that day.

I therefore had to find the courage to face the final half term, and that is what I did. I'd like to think that my bullies became afraid of me because of the way I fought back, but in reality they were probably afraid of what their mothers would do or, worse still, what my mother would do. Either way, they left me alone from that point and some of them even tried to make friends again. I obliged, although I did not forgive or forget. I despised them for thinking stupidly that after all they had done I would be their friend. Determined to dispel any lingering feelings of fear I had of the bullies, I still prayed for them and tried to outwardly show Christian love to them. But hate dominated my true feelings. I know love and hate can never be bedfellows, but it was what I tried to do.

Each day as I walked into school I vowed to show them that I was going be tougher than them, harder, colder and more ruthless. I may have smiled at them with my mouth but my eyes said, 'I hate you.' No one was ever going to touch me again or call me names and get away with it. Things would have to change, perhaps not for the better, but they had to change. If feeling things meant that I was too sensitive then I would not feel. The old me had to be thrown off and a new Claudette had to emerge, one who took no prisoners. Spring had ended, and I decided to take control of my fate; I would never be anyone's victim again.

Summer

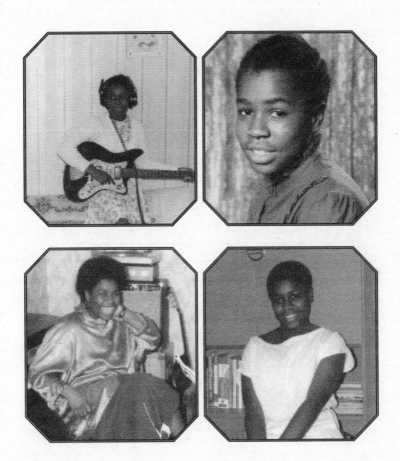

Musical Dream

I had a dream, but not of fame,
One of purity.
I soared up to the highest heights
And set my spirit free.
The caged bird in me flew away,
But couldn't find release.
The dream became the prison
And the song, security.

I walked into a sultry note,
Slid down a silky scale.
I ran along a passionate verse,
And went within the veil.
I saw the notes of peace and hope,
The scale of trust, a sliding slope.
Felt kindness in the passion of voice,
The lyrics of a noble choice.

But I had passion, and no release,
A song, but no melody –
I had the love,
But couldn't find the peace.
It was just a dream it seems.
I had a musical dream.

5
Uncomfortable Heat

Turn to me and be gracious to me, for I am lonely and afflicted.

Psalm 25:16

Upon reaching senior school I vowed to become tough and although I was pleased to leave my old school behind, I didn't trust that I wouldn't get bullied again. Consequently, my first year at my new school was a rocky one and it felt as though I was involved in a fight nearly every week. I had lots of acquaintances but no friends. I tried to shake off the weak victim I had been and I acted strong, but in reality I was scared. I was terrified of being bullied again and was a keg of emotional dynamite ready to go off at any moment. If anyone said one wrong word, swore at me or called me a name, I fought them so that I wouldn't be a victim again. I didn't want to be my father's daughter, but as much as I tried to deny being like him, I was becoming him – angry and aggressive.

The problem I found with trying to be tough was that I cared too much about what people thought of me, and in reality I just wanted people to like me. My first year was eventful and the following summer break proved to be a welcome relief, as I had created even more enemies at my new school than I had before. Fighting was a way of survival but I hated it. It wasn't me, and truth be known I abhorred violence. Every fight made me feel as sick as when I saw my father beat Aunty B.

That summer the evangelist Billy Graham was coming to the city. He was to hold meetings at Villa Park Football Stadium and my mother, who had become a born-again Christian after attending one of our plays at Sunday school and was now a very active church member, was in the choir for the Billy Graham event. Her transformation into a Christian was the best thing that happened to our family, for her prayers have helped to see me through to where I am now, although at the time I could not appreciate it. All her children were ordered to go to the crusades, and we, the kids, had to arrive early with her so that she could rehearse with the choir. As we were early we asked if we could go to the local park with friends before the meeting began and our mother agreed.

Just a few months short of my thirteenth birthday, but still a babe of 12, I tagged along to my older sisters' outing. They knew some teenage boys at the park and of course matchmaking was taking place. Gradually, one by one, the girls we were with paired up with a boy and went off, and eventually my sisters did too. None of the boys we knew liked me, as I was too young for them, and I didn't mind. So I sat on the roundabout wishing the time away by whirling around until my sisters returned so we could go to the meeting.

There was a man, who looked about 19 or 20, who came up to me as I mindlessly swung around. I didn't know him, but he had been a part of the group of lads that my sisters knew, so I thought it would be all right to talk to him. He asked me my name and what I was doing there, and I told him but really didn't say much else. After a short conversation he asked if I wanted to go for a walk and I told him I was waiting for my sisters. He then said he knew where they had gone to and that we could walk that way together. Wanting to relieve the boredom of waiting, I agreed to walk with him. It was a huge mistake because after we walked a short distance we passed the park toilets and he suddenly pulled me inside. There he tried to play the 'game' that I had experienced at my father's flat. I will never forget the smell of his aftershave, which I disliked intensely, and I stood paralysed by fear and by the re-awakening of long-repressed memories from the past. It seemed that every-where I went someone wanted to hurt me. I know that most 12-year-olds today have a lot more knowledge and commonsense than I did back then, but I had an innocent mind when it came to such matters and, instead of fighting him off, I stood frozen to the spot.

It seemed that my lack of reaction worked in my favour because his demeanour changed, and as quickly as he had pulled me into the toilets he pulled me out, and I ran back down to the roundabout where he had found me. By that time my sisters were back and I told them what had just happened; they told me off for leaving with a stranger. I tried to explain that I thought they knew him and that he said he would take me to find them. I held my head down in shame as I was told that I should not have allowed myself to get felt-up. They had only talked to the lads they liked, but I had gone too far. At the time I was unaware of the kind of practices that were commonplace by certain men and women in parks, but I soon learned that this man thought I was one of those types of girls. Special, who was 15 and had a fierce temper, ordered me to point him out. When she found him, as little as she was, she spoke angrily to him, letting him know my age. It seemed so normal to him that anonymous girls would allow him to touch them that he even came up to me and apologized.

'Sorry love, I didn't know, thought you were older,' he said and he patted my cheek as if to say, 'There, there, little girl, it's all better now.'

It was humiliating, and even though nothing as bad as when I was little had happened, and it was over before it begun, the brief incident truly affected me.

Soon it was time to go into the meeting, and my sisters and I ran there quickly. They never mentioned it to me again, but I knew what they thought. It was sluttish behaviour and I was sure they felt that way about me.

As I entered the stadium I was hit by the noise and atmosphere of thousands of people convening to worship. It was a privilege to hear the legendary Billy Graham proclaim the gospel but I could not appreciate the meeting. My mind was consumed and I felt ashamed that I had allowed myself to be taken off in that way. I was guilt-ridden. I wanted the earth to open up and swallow me whole. I wished I was dead, and from then on I withdrew at home. The shame I felt kept me away from my two sisters and 'the kids' were an entity no more. I was not part of them. Sometimes I would overhear them having private conversations without me, and I was sure they were talking about me. I believed that it was my fault because of what I had let that man do. I felt dirty and foolish and began to curse myself as others had.

Since I shared a bedroom with my mother the only private space I had was the bathroom. It became a regular routine for me to sit on the bathroom floor, pull my woolly hat down over my head and hit my head with my fist until it hurt. I felt that I needed punishing and I pinched my arms to feel pain. I wouldn't cry; I just had to hurt me.

Before the incident at the park, I had still been attending the Sunday school that had been my refuge during the bullying years. I had loved it. I loved the songs, the Bible, the activities and, most of all, the worship. I had lived for Sunday until then, but it was at that point that I thought there was no way that God could love me. I had done too many bad things, had too many fights, and now I was deservedly being punished by being hurt. I couldn't understand how God could let these things happen to me. It was summer for me both literally and emotionally, and things were too hot for me to handle, yet I put more coats of protection around my heart in an attempt to block out the agonies I felt. Even so, there was something of the love of God that remained in my heart. I had forgotten the commitment I made when I was 5, but God did not.

The Second Call

Our church used to hold Saturday night revival meetings that were famous across the country. These were powerful meetings, with many healings and miracles taking place, and people would come in coach-loads to Hockley. This also drew some amazing preachers to our small venue in the heart of the city. One Saturday night a gospel singer came to our church. His music was contemporary and it was an evening that was geared towards young people. I went along for the music but halfway through the concert he spoke about a subject very close to my heart. Our church was very open to words of knowledge and prophecy,* and the singer said that there was someone in the meeting who had been bullied. This particular person should come forward to the front to be prayed for as God had a special plan for their life. He said they had turned away from their faith but it was time to recommit. I know the cynic that is in me would say that the statistical probability of a victim of bullying being in a room full of teenagers is high, but this was different. As he spoke I could hear my heart pounding in my ears, and I knew he was talking about me, but I didn't move. I was too afraid and there was no way I was going to get up in front of everyone. So I stayed seated, and when I saw someone else go forward I was relieved. But my relief was short-lived as he thanked them for coming but then spoke further.

'The person God is speaking to is still sitting down and needs to come forward.'

His voice was pleading but authoritative and as I watched yet more people go and stand in front of the platform, he

---

* For those who are unfamiliar with this, these are words that someone speaks in the belief that they have heard directly from God. There are examples and evidence of this all through the Bible.

insisted that the person was still seated. He kept thanking them for coming but was sure that the person concerned had not yet come forward. Finally I could take it no more, as my heart burned in the knowledge it was me. I stood up and went to the front and the gospel singer nodded as if he knew who it was all along, and at that I burst into tears. He then prayed for all the people that came forward, and in prayer I recommitted my life to Christ and asked Jesus to be my friend again. I desperately wanted to change. I didn't want to be the tough, hard and ruthless person I was trying to be – I wanted the love of Jesus, who was a friend to all. I wanted him to take away all the pain I felt and to wash me clean again. It was not the first time that I'd heard that Christ had died for my sins and that he could make my life brand new, but it was the first time that I had been so singled out. God had not forgotten me or left me, and was reaching out to me once again.

After that meeting, when I returned to school the following year and I had changed and was a more sociable person. I even managed to make friends with a girl that I'd had a fight with in my first week at school. Although I was 'once bitten, twice shy' and I don't think I ever really fully trusted her friendship, I held on to it all the same. 'Twice Shy' was the first friend that I'd had in years. I tried to become a kinder person and to let my guard down and eventually a glimpse of the young, happy Claudette began to resurface. It was hard to live down the reputation I had built for myself, and even harder to prove to others that I no longer wanted to fight with everyone. Nevertheless, for the next two years I had no fights or altercations. Each time conflicts arose I tried to resolve them through talking or walking away, which was a hard job in a tough school. Yet God was with me, and peace reigned for those two years. My renewed faith even helped me with my father and I tried to be more patient with him. I prayed that he too would become born again just as my mother had been and then maybe he would stop drinking. His alcoholism had by that point turned his previously immaculate flat into a drunk's den – cards, cigars, magazines and bottles lay strewn everywhere – but I persevered and visited anyway.

I was also in our church's girls' group called the Missionettes, a kind of Pentecostal Girl Guides. We had to memorize scriptures, earn badges and complete tasks, and although I found that I didn't make any close friends whilst there, it didn't matter. It wasn't that they weren't friendly, there simply wasn't time. I was absorbed in the activities. We played games, did arts and crafts, sang songs and generally just had a fun time all based around the faith, good Christian service and charitable deeds. I finally had a respite from the troubles of my childhood and could relax into being a young teenager. By that time I had long attained my prize of my own children's Bible and mine was thoroughly used and worn due to the amount of Scripture we had to memorize in order to get our badges. We even had to commit the whole of 1 Corinthians 13 to memory, and although it was a great big task it was a pleasure because it was all about love and that was what I sought. I highlighted the text in my Bible and eventually the pages became so worn that I had to have a new one.

Each night before I went to bed my mother and I would pray the prayer she had taught to me as a child. 'This night as I lay down to sleep, I pray the Lord my soul to keep. If I should die before I wake, I pray the Lord my soul to take. Heavenly Father hear my cry, Lord protect me through this night; bring me safe till morning light, through Jesus Christ our Lord. Amen.' Then she would pray for the family and for anything else that seemed appropriate, but silently before we said our final 'amen' I would add, *Please Lord, send me a special friend – a best friend.'*

More than anything I wanted someone of my very own, a real friend. Although Twice Shy and I were friends, I never allowed her to be truly close. I couldn't quite trust her enough to let her into my confidence. I certainly couldn't afford to give her any ammunition to use against me if our friendship failed, which I was sure it would. I couldn't believe that anyone would truly like to be friends with me.

During those two years my sister Special and I became closer again as we walked home from school together. I remember the fun of those days as we sang songs in harmony on the way. As we walked we talked about our day, made up stories and told numerous jokes, laughing until we were light-headed. We giggled so much in the summer heat that we couldn't walk straight.

Things were finally looking up, but secretly I began to worry. I was nervous, as the following school year Special would be moving on to college and, once again, I would be at school with no siblings around. I hoped and prayed that I would be alright, but deep down fear began to build up. The scars of the years before had left an invisible, yet apparently indelible mark. Those scars were to influence my future actions, but for a while at least, my time at school was better than before.

When the summer holidays came the initial fear I had began to preoccupy me. I could not shake the feeling that being without family at school meant I was doomed. In my worry I turned to food and in the solitary hours of the holidays I ate. I ate for comfort and companionship; I ate for pleasure. The puppy fat that I had long worn was now turning into rotund plumpness. The ravages of teenage hormones meant that my skin broke out in eczema and no amount of make-up could hide the damage it was doing to my face. I compared myself to my sisters and internally proclaimed myself the 'ugly duckling'.

The Long, Hot Summer

When I returned to school after that summer things had definitely changed. I was fatter, and it seemed to me that I was uglier than everyone else. It was further proved to be the case when all my friends had a boyfriend apart from me. Twice Shy started to go out with a 16-year-old student. We were in the year below and had not even turned 15, so her going out with him was a definite coup. Not only was he older than her, he was also one of the bad boys of the school. He, 'Rough' (in all senses of the word), and his sister, 'Ready' (who was in my year), had only recently come to the school and instinctively my guard was up. Rough was arrogant to the extreme and Ready was another 'New Girl'. The minute she started to compete for Twice Shy's friendship I knew I was fighting a losing battle. So, anticipating confrontation, I decided to give them all a wide berth in order to avoid any jealousies. I didn't know it, but this was the first time I used the tactic that was later to become my strategy of choice – to reject others before they rejected me. It was a strategy doomed to failure but in the light of subsequent events it was probably the best thing to have done. I'd make excuses that I had to be some-where else at break times and find a quiet place by myself and read, just so I wouldn't have to face the possibility of rejection.

Whilst I was absent from my friends, however, a new gang, or 'posse' as they were called, was forming, with Rough and Ready at the centre of the group. Whenever I did spend the odd break time with them I felt out of place; they called me posh because I didn't swear or behave like them, and especially because I went to church.

That should have been my cue to keep well clear of the group, but after my previous experience of bullying I craved the acceptance of my peers, even though they were nothing like me and it was obvious that I was a 'church girl'. Scared that my discreet distancing would be perceived as being stuck-up, acceptance became my main goal. I feared rejection more than anything else that had happened to me in the past and so I tried to fit in to their culture.

Very slowly, little by little, I began to join in as I was afraid of being ostracized again. At first I gave myself lim-its and tried to pretend that I was part of the crowd, taking just the odd puff of Twice Shy's cigarette here or there at break times. Rough would watch me and laugh, as he knew

I wasn't really inhaling. One day he made me inhale fully and as I coughed, he laughed. I was embarrassed but I knew I had to impress this boy in order to be one of the posse, so instead of just the odd cigarette I joined them in their outings. This meant truanting from school, smoking cigarettes and drinking alcohol.

I tried to maintain an element of my faith and thought that I should draw the line at something, so I decided that I wouldn't swear. I felt it still distinguished me as a Christian and I believed in my heart that it was my way of keeping the faith. But 'the heart is deceitful above all things' (Jer. 17:9). I was soon to discover that even in the heat of summer I could be ice cold. The warmth of the Son of God was being blocked out by more protective coats – deception, secrecy and fear. I was 14 years old and living a double life; a good church girl at home, going to Sunday school and Missionettes, yet all the while shoplifting, smoking and drinking alcohol when I was supposed to be at school. My double life was going well, or so I thought, until a few weeks in when I was to make the worst decision of my life. Things were about to become far too hot for me to handle.

6
Mad About The Boy

Folly . . . says, 'Stolen water is sweet; food eaten in secret is delicious!.' But little do they know that the dead are there, that her guests are deep in the realm of the dead.

Proverbs 9:17–18

I felt different and inadequate in comparison to my friends, and I didn't think it was because of my faith. I believed it was because I had never had a boyfriend. And even though I'd had experiences a child should never have to go through, I still wanted one. Too ashamed to tell my peers about my experiences, I lied and concocted a past so elaborate with boyfriends galore that I now see how foolish I must have looked. I tried to convince the streetwise, knowledgeable youths around me that I was not as ignorant or as innocent as I seemed – but I was.

Twice Shy and Rough had been an established couple for a number of months and I had thoroughly convinced myself that the only way to remedy the differences between myself and the group was to get a boyfriend. The boy I chose was Rough's best friend. The added kudos for me was that he was in the same year as Rough and therefore I would potentially be going out with an older boy, giving me immediate street credibility. He was good-looking, not very tall and, being of Caribbean-Arabian descent, he had reddish brown skin and soft curly hair; he was everything I wasn't. I felt ugly, while he was handsome, nicer than Rough and seemed more intelligent, and I soon became mad about 'The Boy'. Before long I let Twice Shy know that I liked him and we, in our girly way, let him know with all the subtlety of a brick. I hoped that if I went out with him Rough would accept me as part of the group. Before long, romantic notions abounded in my young mind and I saw us as a great foursome, two couples who were all best friends. Twice Shy acted as intermediary and within days I had my first official boyfriend, although technically he had not asked me out. I had done the asking by way of letter and the customary tick boxes, and I couldn't believe it when he said yes. I was to learn that this was a big mistake.

At first the relationship with The Boy was sweet, as I had imagined it to be. We passed little notes to each other and later had our first walk. He never said that I was pretty, or that he liked me, but I was still smitten. By the end of the week we got together he walked me home from school and we had our first kiss. We exchanged phone numbers and each time we talked I felt that we had like minds and a lot in common. Of course, our phone calls had to be kept secret and take place before my mother got home from work, as I was strictly forbidden from having a boyfriend – as were all the girls in the family, in fact. Nevertheless, he was my first boyfriend and I was sure that after we became an established couple I would truly be part of the posse. I therefore ignored my mother's ruling. My plan seemed to work, as I noticed that even Rough began to nod at me and sometimes say hello, whereas before he never even acknowledged my presence, apart from giving the odd derisory comment. Theirs was a tough group to get into, and I didn't understand how far apart our minds were when it came to acceptance, but Twice Shy and I had been friends for two years and I wanted to keep her.

After a week or so of seeing The Boy he changed towards me. He was still friendly and even charming, but with his charm came intense pressure. Day after day he would pressure me to go to my house when the family was out, or better still I should come back to his. I refused, as although I was naive I wasn't stupid, and from past experience I knew what could happen. I was not going down that path again and believed that if he truly cared for me, he would respect my wishes. He was 16 years old and more experienced, however, and I should have realized that that was all he wanted from me.

Although I had 'backslidden', as some Christians would term it, as I had come away from the practices of the faith, in my heart I still believed and still tried to portray the image of a good Christian at home. However, I found all the secrets increasingly hard to keep from my family. Secrecy was now the enemy that I had befriended, and I had kept quiet about so many things in my life that this was now normal. I wanted to prove to my family that I could cope by myself and that I wasn't too sensitive. I believed that changing my behaviour to fit in was the only way to gain acceptance, however, and before long even my duplicity stopped; I was less concerned about keeping up the front of the 'good Christian girl'. At first I skipped my beloved girls' group, the Missionettes, but eventually I told my mother that I no longer wanted to go. I could see the disappointment in her face, especially when I told her I no longer wanted to go to Sunday school either. All my siblings had long stopped attending and I was getting too old for it, I argued. She agreed, however I was told I still had to go to church on Sunday mornings. Although I complied, my heart was far removed from the now seemingly staid and irrelevant church meetings that didn't seem to say anything but condemn sinners to hell and give crowns to the victors.

From then on I embarked on a downward spiral of smoking, drinking and, finally, back to my old behaviour of fighting. The tough Claudette had necessarily re-emerged as my assimilation into the culture of my peers led to the inevitable arguments as we vied for position and supremacy. The vanity of youth is one of image and how others perceive us, and every day I absorbed that vanity just so I could fit in. I no longer attended the majority of my lessons at school and my education suffered badly. The Boy and I would skip classes and go for walks or bus rides. I imagined myself to be in love, or something like it, with this young, handsome but, unbeknown to me, insincere guy.

He pressured me continuously about going to his house and one day I opted for a walk to a local park instead, but all the way there he talked about 'it' and how I should 'be with' him. Apparently, Twice Shy had already 'been with' Rough and The Boy's barely concealed euphemisms were becoming difficult to ignore. I was hurt that Twice Shy hadn't told me about it, but our friendship had already started to fall apart. She was now closer friends with Ready, and I was holding on to my membership of the posse by the thinnest of threads – The Boy.

The pressure increased and as I came up with more excuses as to why I couldn't be with him I knew it had become a big issue between us. When we got to the park we sat down to share a cigarette but didn't speak. Knowing that my refusals were wearing thin on him, I stuttered feeble excuses of having stuff to do at home. At this he tried to talk me around, and although I didn't want to admit to being a virgin, I eventually made him understand that I had never done anything like that before and that I wouldn't be persuaded. Immediately the conversation and pressure stopped; he changed the subject abruptly and suggested we go our separate ways home via an old pavilion. At first I thought I had upset him but as we walked he discussed the latest music and even cracked a joke or two.

It was the end of the day and I had hardly been at school but had to maintain the pretence by getting home at the right time. I was about to say goodbye as we had reached the pavilion but then The Boy asked if I would be comfortable with just a kiss. I was happy that he finally understood that I wanted a boyfriend but nothing too physical, and together we stepped inside the ramshackle porch. He put out his cigarette and his smile caught me off guard. If I had looked closer I would have seen the intent in his eyes as he sarcastically said that a kiss was all I was to give and receive and stepped towards me. I closed my eyes awaiting his kiss but soon realized something was amiss and opened them to look down. What I saw horrified me. He was lifting my skirt. In panic I tried to push him away, but before I knew it I was pinned to the wall, trapped, with my arms held down. This time I knew I had to fight so I tried to kick him, but it was useless, he was too strong. The next few minutes were a blur and like a limp rag doll I flopped in blank submission. I didn't think about what was happening to me but instead thought of how I had disobeyed my mother and got a boyfriend, skipped school, lied, cheated and stolen, so now I deserved everything I got.

When the torment ended he stepped away from me and the look in my eyes told him I was destroyed. I will never forget the way he smiled and calmly lit a cigarette. It felt as if he was saying, 'That'll teach you to say no to me.' He started to talk and from what I could gather he believed that what had just occurred was part of a rite of passage in our relationship. According to him, all my protestations were part of the elaborate game that girls played. My 'no' meant 'no', yet he thought I was joking and saw it as a challenge. He was pleased and I was disgusted. He had fought with me to get his way, and I was shocked to hear that he thought that we were still a couple. To my astonishment he even boasted that I must have enjoyed what he had done. I spoke, albeit incoherently, and tried to maintain an appearance of normality as he said goodbye and walked away.

I remained there frozen, completely frozen. I don't know what time it was when I finally walked home. All the way I felt like crying, but no tears would come. It was as though someone had put an icicle on my heart and it was dirty and cold, bitterly cold. I don't remember letting myself in through the door, but I do remember that my sisters were upstairs so, not wanting them to see me, I went into the kitchen. I sat down by the heater and hugged myself, shaking with the cold, trying to cry, but no tears would come. I shivered and rocked back and forth until I told myself to stop, but I couldn't, so I punched my legs and started banging my head against the wall in order to block out the thoughts of the attack. All the names of the past came flooding back: 'Bouncer', 'Fatty' and every evil label that I had ever been given came to me, but it was me doing the name calling. I insulted and reviled myself as I felt I was to blame.

In my mind I tried to go back to the happiest times I'd had, back to Saturday mornings with the music, laughter and family time; swirling around the living room hand-in-hand with my mother, with me singing at the top of my voice. The only thing I could think to do was sing. I had always loved singing, but that was the day that singing became an essential part of my survival. I felt I had no one to turn to and certainly didn't want to pray. I didn't think God would hear me anyway. I couldn't tell my sisters as I remembered how they had reacted after the park incident and I certainly couldn't tell my mother as I wasn't even supposed to have a boyfriend. So instead I told it in a song. I stopped rocking and went upstairs to the bathroom to wash, and on the way I sang in an effort to block out the memory of the sexual assault. Music played in my head, and I sang loud and hard. Anyone listening would have thought I was happy but I was not. I was devastated, but my only way out was a fantasy world of singing and pretence.

I scrubbed until I was red raw in an effort to peel the feeling of The Boy away from me. Once I had drowned out the thoughts in singing, I calmly called The Boy and told him that I couldn't go out with him any more. From the way he had talked in the pavilion I knew that he thought I was still going to be his girlfriend, but there was no way I could carry on. Trying to be part of the posse was not worth that kind of pain and I had to sever the relationship with both him and the gang. He asked if I was breaking up with him because of what he did and I lied, answering no. At that he sniggered. Hearing him laugh made me realize that he didn't care for me at all, and I hung up the phone. As I did, it dawned on me that the very thing that I had tried to keep precious from him was what had spurred him on – it was a game of conquests and he had won.

I felt numb at my stupidity, but I determined not to be too sensitive about it. I knew other girls had done the same thing and even wondered if I was making a big deal about nothing. Maybe it was a rite of passage – but it was not one that I wanted to take. Feeling sick from the phone call, I went downstairs to the living room to play music and drown out every thought that plagued me. I sang along with my favourites – Whitney Houston, Chaka Khan, Stevie Wonder and the Eurhythmics – and with all manner of songs, all in a bid to erase the memories of the attack. But nothing could take that ice-cold feeling away from me, even though I sang longer and louder. When my mother came home she must have thought that it was to a teenager who was wrapped up in music, having a good time. She smiled, and when I got too loud told me to 'stop my noise' and laughed lovingly. To all outward appearances I was happy, but on the inside I was dying. So when I couldn't sing aloud I mimed whilst listening on headphones and imagined standing on stage, singing to thousands of adoring fans, all of them loving me and saying how wonderful I was. It wasn't really me – yet that was the point. I didn't want to be me: in my fantasy I was a slim, beautiful singer with an immaculate past and a wonderful future.

Comfort Food

The following day at school I knew I had to do my own kind of public relations in order to retain some kind of credibility, so when I saw Twice Shy I lied and told her that my mother had found out about my relationship and that was why I had to finish with The Boy. I also said that I would be staying away from them all for a while because it would be awkward to see him again regularly. She gave me a wry knowing smile and pretended to be surprised, but it was obvious that she wasn't. The Boy must have told them all, because over the next few days I found that my name was being bandied around and I was getting funny looks from people in my class.

I began to skip school more often or would arrive late and make up lame excuses. I felt ostracized once more, and my fear of The Boy and of being bullied overwhelmed me. I wore long cardigans and coats to cover the body that I was ashamed of as I turned to food for comfort. My favourite was chocolate. I would eat up to four bars a day as well as my usual food. I knew no boundaries when it came to eating and became moody and quiet. My weight increased and there seemed to be nothing I could do about it as I had tried dieting but struggled. My sisters were all very slim but I was size 16 and growing. Within a short while I was bigger than my mother, a woman who'd had seven children.

I remember coming home from church one day in a foul mood and was very quiet until after I had eaten, and then I cheered up. At that my sister Pearl told me off in front of the family, saying that I was greedy and behaved badly, as I was sulking just because of food. It was then that I felt the full humiliation of my eating and, even if it was not intended, I took it to mean that once again I was different. They were all skinny and no one in my family was overweight except for me. I couldn't tell anyone why I was eating so much. I didn't even really know why myself – I just knew that I felt better when I ate. I suppose that was when I began to associate guilt with my eating and started to eat in secret so that no one could see what I was doing. I didn't want to be judged or humiliated like that again. The spring blossoms of fear, mistrust and abuse had now fully formed. Added to the outfits of silence and secrecy I put on summer coats of guilt, self-loathing and hate, and together they fashioned my outlook on life. I believed the worst of people because they had abused and taunted me, and I despised them all.

The Writing on the Wall

The school was located on a mile-long straight road with rows of houses and just before a crossroads to the depressing state building, there was a long red-brick wall. One morning, about a week after the assault, my sister Serene and I happened to be travelling on the same bus. She was on her way to college, which was not far from my school, and we sat together as I gazed out of the window of the top deck, dreading yet another lonely day. The bus stopped along the route and I peered at the houses, trying to plot my plan of action and avoidance for the day ahead, but as I looked through the dirty glass window, my heart dropped a beat. Graffitied along the six-foot-high red-brick wall, written in enormous capital letters, spray painted in white, were the words:

'CLAUDETTE ***** IS A FAT *****'

My full name was on view for the world to see, and no doubt every child on their way to school that morning had seen it too. It was huge and clearly visible from a distance. Serene saw it and was shocked, and instead of going to college came into the school with me. I let my sister deal with the matter in the appropriate way, and she went to find the deputy head teacher, but secretly I had my own plan for dealing with it. I knew what had to be done. I didn't cry but resigned myself to the fact that the bullying was to begin again. I thought I recognized the penmanship on the wall and believed it to be a certain fringe member of the posse, who was notorious for those kinds of antics. I should have been afraid, but instead I felt the same rage that I had when New Girl slapped me.

It was morning break time and the hall was full of children buying tuck and chatting. I saw the person I believed to be responsible for the graffiti and, focusing my rage and hate towards him, I calmly walked up to him and punched him on the back of his head. Chaos broke loose as we fought, and the teacher and Serene ran out of the office as the hall erupted in chants of 'Fight, fight!' and I was pulled off the boy. Tears finally fell, but they were of anger, not fear, and I was sent home.

Later, when Serene got home she told me that the teacher had decided not to suspend me and that I could go back to school the next day. When I did return she gave me a very stern talking to, but she was also very kind as she had gone down to the wall with some of the older students and washed off the graffiti. I felt the kindness of her actions, as what I had done should have earned me a week's suspension automatically. Unfortunately the damage of the graffiti had already been done. I was now known throughout school as the 'fat b****', and I was even pointed out to those who didn't know me. The gang that I had tried so desperately to be part of became my enemies, and Twice Shy and I stopped speaking.

Once again I was alone in school, with no friends to whom I could talk. Needless to say, my school work suffered terribly during this time. I don't remember handing in a single piece of homework, yet the teachers were very patient and gave me a lot of latitude. I wanted to learn, but found it impossible in school. The bullying that I suffered in senior school was more about isolation. I was sent to Coventry; no one wanted to be friends with me. I ate alone, walked alone, and was alone. I lived in a world of songs, books and food. I couldn't pray as I believed that after what had happened with The Boy there was no way God was on my side.

Running for My Life

It became my routine at the end of the school day to wait until the people I thought disliked me had got on their buses and that usually meant I caught the emptiest bus. One afternoon as I came out of the school gates I was surprised to see about a dozen or so people at the bus stop, but there was no one from the gang so I thought it would be safe to wait there. Two teenage boys were arguing, which was nothing unusual at that school, and I leaned against a wall to watch the drama unfold – and it certainly did. Gradually the argument escalated until one boy took out a knife and stabbed the other in the leg. The stabbing victim was a white boy whose skin went so deathly pale that I could tell he was going to pass out, and he did. The wound wasn't very deep, but there was enough blood for an ambulance to be called. As soon as the bus came I jumped aboard quickly while a crowd gathered around the spectacle.

At school the following day I saw Twice Shy with some other girls, and as I walked past them I overheard them talking about the stabbing. Whilst eavesdropping I plucked up the courage to tell them that I witnessed it and they asked me what had happened. Amazingly, I still sought their acceptance and was pleased I had their full attention, as I bragged about what I had seen the night before. Unbeknown to me Rough was prowling like a wolf as I told Twice Shy and my former friends the story of the stabbing. I stopped talking when I felt a burning sensation at the back of my neck. Putting my hand to my neck to find out what it was, I yelped in shock when Rough grabbed my hand and held it down. He laughed and continued to do so as he pressed a lit cigarette into my neck, using me as an ashtray. When it was completely out I could smell my flesh burning. He then let go of my hand, quickly took out a flick knife and held it up to my throat. The cold metal reminded me of The Boy's hands, and I shook at the memory of the assault that I thought I had managed to block out. I trembled and waited for him to begin the first cut, closing my eyes.

'You're next,' he said, and then laughed again. 'See you after school.' Then he pushed me aside and let me go. He had only held the knife to my throat for a few seconds but it felt longer. I ran away and, as I did, heard them laughing at me. I turned to look back and saw The Boy. He was watching and his face displayed the contempt he felt for me.

At the end of the day I was afraid to use the same bus stop as the night before, so I walked to one further away. I had made it through the day and lessons by hiding in my usual corners, and all I had to do was get home safely. However, as I walked up the road there was a crowd of around twenty teenagers waiting for me. I immediately turned back but they spotted me and followed me. This was not the same posse, but they knew who I was and my name was now down as a target for all. They physically manhandled me. With each push it got harder to walk and I tripped as they shoved me down the road. My hair was pulled, names were called, my body poked and jabbed, but worse than that was they called me the name from junior school. One of the boys had been to my old school and he led the group in their abuse and called me Bouncer once again. Then he said I shouldn't come to school the next day, as they would cut me if I did.

A stranger passing by heard the commotion and told them to leave me alone. He was a middle-aged man and the group stared him down, but he didn't care. He asked if I was OK, although I didn't answer, and the group left. It was as though a guardian angel had been sent. I looked at the man but said nothing and just took flight and ran home. I could no longer keep the bullying and abuse a secret; in fear of a threat on my life, I had to get out of that school. I had kept quiet about it because I didn't want to be seen as weak, but that evening I showed my sister Special the burn marks on my neck and she dragged me to my mother. I told her about the knife threats, but not the assault as it was something I was too ashamed to mention. I was immediately pulled out of the school and within two weeks I was transferred. There was no question of me ever returning.

Going to another school was a frightening prospect, and I resigned myself, expecting that I would be bullied again, hurt again and abused again, so I dressed for the winter that I thought would come. My fate was sealed and my character formed. I had literally seen the writing on the wall and it proclaimed me a 'fat b****'. It foretold a future of pain and hurt, and I was ready to embrace whatever would come next. I had no hopes of it getting better and truly expected the worst.

7
Lost in Music

Like one who takes away a garment on a cold day, or like vinegar poured on a wound, is one who sings songs to a heavy heart.

Proverbs 25:20

I joined a new school halfway through my fourth year of senior school. I was 15 years old and a new system of qualifications was starting, the GCSEs. My year group was to be the first to do this kind of course. Previously most subjects were exam-driven, however with the new system it would be a combination of coursework and exams. The problem was that I was so far behind on so many subjects that I was lost when I sat in class for the first time; I had done no coursework whatsoever. I remember that one of my first lessons was English and I was completely bewildered as the students interacted with the teacher. They knew words and terms that I didn't understand, which made me feel scared and intellectually inept.

I tried to hide my fear of the strange young people around me, but I needn't have worried for they were nothing like Rough, Ready or Twice Shy. At the Church of England school I was with some very unusual young people. They were intelligent, vibrant and, weirdly enough, quite a few of them were Christians. They weren't as exuberant as people from my church; most of them had a much quieter faith. They were also very different from the students at my old school for they were kind and didn't look at me with suspicion as the new girl; they even introduced themselves, welcoming me into their class. It was quite a shock to receive such acceptance and I have to say that I was extremely wary of it.

One of the girls in my class I shall call 'Angel', as she acted like a true messenger sent from God. Angel was a traditional High-Church Anglican who loved the formality of bells and smells, and all the pomp and ceremony. I had always attended a mixed congregational, modern charismatic church, and many of the black people I knew attended black-led churches with similar beliefs. Angel was black but Anglican to the core and it was through my friendship with her that I experienced another aspect of Christianity, with an emphasis on an understated but practical, compassionate belief. There was little mention of spiritual gifts, healing and miracles, which I had heard about for many years in my home church. Angel embraced her faith with such calm assurance that it quite disturbed me. She did not seem to have the battle within that I was having and, because of this, I think she took pity on me. She made it her mission to befriend me but although we talked and she helped me with my school work, I always held back. I decided to enjoy her company but expect nothing in return and firmly believed that our friendship could and would fall apart. I didn't trust her, as it was my experience that betrayal always followed friendship and, after that, bullying.

I became even more lost in music and threw myself into singing. Instead of doing homework I would sing for hours each night, and it became my refuge. When I sang my thoughts couldn't plague me and no one could harm me in my land of fantasy. I would pretend to be someone else, mainly Whitney Houston of whom I was, and still am, a great fan. My brother Art continued to spoil me and took me to my first major concert; the great diva herself was in the country and I went to hear her perform. To say she was astounding would have undervalued the impact that concert had on my life. From the moment she walked onto the stage at the National Exhibition Centre she was mesmerizing. When the beautiful woman opened her mouth to sing I grew faint at the exquisite tone and power of her voice.

My fate was sealed there and then and my passion for singing increased after hearing Whitney. I knew that it was the only thing I wanted to do. I saw the adoration that she received from fans as they screamed her name and told her that they loved her. People loved her for her voice, and I wanted them to love me for mine, so I began to sing around the school. Always humming a tune, I soon got a reputation as the 'girl with the voice'. Singing was my life and became central to my personality. I wanted it to speak for me because it seemed whenever anyone got to know the real me, they soon came to despise me; they would never love me for me. Singing gave me the identity I wanted and it overshadowed the ugly, fat girl I felt I was. When my friends heard me sing they loved it and although I knew I wasn't being accepted for me, I didn't blame them, for I didn't accept me either. It was my way of winning friends and influencing people.

As it was an Anglican school the students attended services regularly and when we were privileged to have the Archbishop Desmond Tutu come to the city, our school was to take part in a concert for him. In preparation for this I was asked to sing 'Amazing Grace' at the Easter service for the school. Unfortunately, after the bullying of my former years I had developed a fear of people looking at me, and this manifested itself at the Easter service. I was so scared that Angel had to hold my hand and stand next to me while I sang. I couldn't even open my eyes, as the thought of people looking at me was terrifying. Yet, in spite of this, there was a desire to perform and when I opened my mouth to sing it felt as though I were lifted out of myself and into another place.

The words of the song meant little to me. Amazing grace? I did not think that God's grace was amazing. If it was, then why had he allowed so many bad things to happen to me? But even with these thoughts I sang with passion and at 15 years of age, for the first time, my mother heard me sing a whole song instead of just bursts of one pop chorus or another. Astonished that her little girl really could sing, she invested in singing lessons for me. At the time I didn't appreciate them, however, as my tutor's style was very operatic and I was made to sing old songs about flowers, with old-fashioned lyrics and motifs – not the kind of thing an aspiring soul singer wanted to sing.

Daddy's Downfall

After my mother became a born-again Christian my sister Pearl also found faith and we all went together to church. It was a regular family outing, and changed the situation with regard to visiting my father. The weekends at my father's became just Sunday afternoon visits, especially when my mother started to go to church for what seemed to be every day of the week. He was by no means happy about it but, as Sunday morning church attendance was now compulsory in the family, it suited me just fine.

By the time I got to his flat on Sunday afternoons I would find him well on his way to being drunk. To complete his drunken state, and possibly to show his displeasure at my lateness, he would make me go to the betting shop with him. Sitting on the floor of the smoky and testosterone-filled bookies while he placed his bets was an unpleasant experience, but not as unpleasant as where we visited afterwards. An abiding memory I have is that whether he won or lost at the bookies, we would go to the pub afterwards. It was not the kind of family-friendly establishment that we see in Britain today. Back in the 1980s the pubs my father frequented were not what one would call child-friendly, so he had a ruse to get me in.

He pretended that I was his girlfriend.

Even though small in stature, at 15 years old, with a well-developed figure, and when dressed in my Sunday best, I passed for 18. I received the worst kind of education about the male of the species as I stood beside my father while he drank himself senseless. Unable to leave, I tried to make myself invisible by crumpling my shoulders, trying to hide my figure, but there was no point. Lecherous old men would ogle and make lewd comments, and some even tried to touch me. It was not the kind of thing that my father would have stood for when sober, but when drunk anything could happen, and sometimes did. I was not as naive as I once had been, and the things that were said to me were revolting, but in his drunken state my father would laugh it off. He seemed proud to show off a supposedly young girlfriend, putting his hand around my waist. I felt sick. I wasn't his girlfriend. I was his daughter.

When we finally returned to his flat and my visit ended he would put one or two pounds in my hands, as though I were some kind of cheap escort with whom he had just finished dealing. As he slumped on the sofa I was ordered to call my brother to come and pick me up. I was disgusted but when I went home I didn't say anything, as I was now an expert at covering up. He behaved this way for a few weeks until my mother, after noticing a change in me, started to ask in-depth questions about my visits. It took a while for me to open up but eventually I told her the bare facts about what was happening, although I didn't tell her how I truly felt – I felt cheap, degraded and at times I hated my father. The bare facts were appalling enough, though, and my mother was outraged; I was not supposed to go to pubs, especially the ones that my father frequented. She told me I didn't have to go to visit him any more if I didn't want to but I worried that he might discontinue the child support that he so infrequently gave.

'The Lord will provide' was her last word on the subject and from then on my visits became less frequent. I would go occasionally but each visit was timed and I would leave within a couple of hours, not giving him enough time to take me anywhere unsuitable. Whilst there I would busy myself trying to clean his flat and we hardly spoke. My father had changed and so had I. I was no longer the little girl he had once adored, and he didn't seem to know what to do with me.

In a bid for acceptance but also revenge I decided to change my name by deed poll. Up until the age of 16 I had always had my father's surname, but I felt it singled me out from my siblings. I no longer wanted to be my father's daughter – well, not the daughter of the father that he had become. My mother agreed, as by this time his behaviour was becoming more aggressive, so I took on the name of her ex-husband instead, the same name as my brothers and sisters.

My father was not the man I once knew and was constantly drunk. I couldn't bear to be around him, so my mother and I went to the registrar, paid the nominal fee and the deed was done. It felt like an initiation into the family; now I was officially the same as everyone else in the house. I would belong with them and not with him, which was all I wanted. But when my father found out that I had changed my name he went ballistic, not at me but at my mother. Another argument ensued, but it was done; it had hurt him and I was pleased. I had wanted to get back at him for the degrading pub visits and I disowned his name. This was something that I later discovered he would never forgive and my infrequent visits were uncomfortable. He was a drunk and I hated what drink did to him – yet strangely enough, although I found it hard to respect him, deep down I still loved him. He was my daddy and the only one I had.

Summer's Cool-Down

For a couple of years at least, my life was uneventful in the respect that it settled into some kind of normality. My final year and a half at school was peaceful and quiet. I was not popular or in a gang, but I wasn't bullied and for me that was all that mattered. Although I liked some boys at school I never let a crush develop beyond a thought and was determined never to have a boyfriend. I made a solemn vow that I would never allow anyone to touch me again. I decided to concentrate on my school work and catch up with my class-mates. They all seemed to have career paths ahead of them: some wanted to be doctors, others teachers, solicitors or various other professions. I had never before met young people with such high ambitions. Even though I was bright, I had missed too much of my education and wasn't expected to do well in my exams. This hurt deeply, as I envied the choices my friends had. Once again, a sense of inadequacy overwhelmed me but I tried to throw it all aside and concentrate on singing.

My brother Art continued to be a friend, taking me along with him to motor shows and events, but pretty soon my interests changed. Music became everything. My eldest brother Indie moved back into the family home after his relationship with his long-term partner faltered. His humour was infectious and I enjoyed his company. My relationship with my sisters soured, however, as my moods swung like a pendulum; I was consumed with the paranoid belief that they were talking about me. I felt isolated and, although I had taken the family name, in heart I felt I would never truly be one of them. I think that is why I liked Indie so much because he was a half-ling too, having been born in Barbados before my mother married my other siblings' father. He had my mother's maiden name, and if I had thought better I should probably have taken that one, which may not have offended my father so much.

After nearly two years at the school I still had only one proper friend – Angel. Like me, she had been a person of faith all her life, but one day she called me and told me that she had become a 'born-again' Christian. I sighed in dismay as I knew what it meant; I had seen the transformation in my own family with my mother and sister. It gave her renewed passion for the faith, which was great to see. I understood and remembered it well, but I couldn't get into it. My faith was now non-existent and I didn't believe God cared for me.

It was April, I was 16 years old and for me the exam season was over very quickly. I was only taking two subjects, having failed the rest of my coursework. After my second and final exam I vowed that I would never go back into a school again; I didn't even return to get my certificates for the two low-graded GCSEs I had managed to attain. Even though the people there hadn't been bad to me, I hated the very institution called school. I hated the buildings, the system and everything it stood for. However, hating and rejecting the past can often lead to a lack of direction for the future, and I didn't know what to do with myself. I knew I wanted to be a singer but there were no opportunities – not for a girl of my size and looks.

I had stopped attending all church services some time ago, as I didn't seem to get much out of them, but something or

Someone was drawing me back. Mom was now on a personal crusade to see all of her children saved and following God, so she tried to persuade me to go back. As I had nothing better to do, I agreed – though I wasn't sure why.

Three Strikes

When I went to bed at night I had terrible nightmares about the past, as events in my early life continued to trouble me. They would play as though on an old projector, one frame at a time, slowly torturing me so that I couldn't sleep. In the daytime I would hear the voices of the bullies in my head, swearing and calling me names. In my dreams The Boy would appear and I would relive the assault. I blamed myself for everything. It got so bad that one night I tried to stop breathing, placing my head in the pillow and wanting to black out and never wake up. The mental torture was excruciating.

The only time I felt peaceful was when I was at church, although the words of the preacher didn't do anything for me, as each Sunday I heard sermons on how God had a purpose for our lives, yet I couldn't see one in mine at all. There was respite from my nightmares whilst I was there, however, and it became my Sunday piece of heaven again. The memories of my childhood prayers came flooding back and I recalled when I had asked God to be my friend at just 5 years old and again at 12.

After a few weeks of going back to church I felt the urge to talk to God again. I had never doubted his existence and believed he could hear me but I wasn't sure if he would. I had abandoned my faith and didn't think God would forgive that.

Once I had left school I didn't go out on weekdays, as I had no career prospects and lived in constant fear, terrified of life and my future. With no decent qualifications, going to college or university wasn't an option for me and my future looked bleak. Nightmares continued to plague me and made me very confused. This led me to the verge of a nervous breakdown. Suicidal thoughts played on my mind and each day I contemplated whether to let death take me over. I was tempted to talk to Angel about it, as I envied her faith. She was full of joy and love, but I couldn't talk to her because I was sure that she only felt that way because she wasn't as bad a sinner as I.

My lack of understanding of God's grace showed and I struggled. I wanted to be a friend of God but could not forgive myself for allowing bad things to happen. Daily I felt his call, once again, just as I had done when the gospel singer came to the church. I felt desperate for God to be in my life, so one evening at home I knelt next to the sofa in the kitchen and asked the Lord to forgive me again, to take me back to the first time I put my hand up and asked him to be my friend. I talked to him the only way I knew how, which was through song, and sang the old Andrae Crouch song 'Take Me Back', wanting to rekindle my faith and start anew.

When I finished I nervously went upstairs and told my mother that I wanted to be born again and she prayed with me. I truly thought that it would resolve all the issues I had, but I was to come to understand that salvation itself is a continuous process (see Titus 3:4–6), although I wanted instant results. I wanted that Pentecostal, Damascus Road, Apostle Paul experience where everything changed instantaneously (see Acts 9). If I had read further on in my Bible I would have seen the Apostle Paul's process as well and how he struggled and suffered, but I was 16 and I saw things only one way – the quick and easy way.

Not understanding the journey of faith I was on, I struggled with the ghosts of the past that kept haunting me and my faith wavered constantly. I made a commitment but found it hard to keep and I wasn't quite sure what God wanted from me. I was at a crossroads and knew I had to make up my mind one way or another, as I didn't fully trust the God who supposedly made the heavens and earth and sent his Son to die so that I could live. I certainly didn't trust his ability to stop me from getting hurt again. Hurt and angry, I wanted his peace but was terrified of his love. From what I could hear at church the main emphasis each Sunday was total surrender and dependence on God, and I thought I had done that before and it hadn't helped. My fear of being let down meant that I decided to let God into my life to a certain degree, but some things were still mine. I became a Christian, but I still wanted to keep my own coats of protection – just in case it all went wrong again.

A few months later it was advertised in the newspapers that the evangelist Reinhard Bonnke was to hold a crusade at the National Exhibition Centre in Birmingham, the same venue where I had seen Whitney Houston in concert. I had heard about the preacher when I was younger and knew of his work in Africa, but for some reason when I read he was coming I felt a burning desire to attend. I couldn't explain why but I knew I had to be at that meeting, so I asked my mother to take me and we took the train to the NEC. It was Sunday 24 July 1988, and as we arrived at the arena I was overwhelmed by the sheer number of people there – more than there had been at the Whitney concert. The place heaved with people of all nations, ages and, it seemed, persuasions. We quickly found seats and waited for the meeting to start. When it did I have to admit to being a little disappointed. Not that it wasn't good, as they sang worship songs that I knew and the atmosphere was electric. I found it rather formulaic, however, and had been hoping for something different because of the feeling I'd had. I couldn't understand why I felt so strongly that I had to be there when it was just the same as every other Christian meeting I had been to. They usually began with praise before worship (fast, then slow songs), then testimonies, the soloist and finally the preacher. I knew the formula well and sang along as a matter of routine. At the point when the soloist came on I started to wonder if I was really meant to be there, as nothing amazing had happened.

We took our seats as a young lady got up to sing, and to this day I cannot remember the name of the girl or the song that she sang. All I know is that as she sang, something wonderful happened. Whereas before songs were a means of escape into a fantasy world, the song and the way she sang it made everything seem real. Every word, note and scale seemed to pull at my heart. Even though Whitney had inspired a passion for singing in me, this woman's voice had something that I could not explain. My mother called it the 'anointing', a special gift from God. I didn't know what it was but I knew that it wasn't her vocal prowess that touched me. She was no Whitney by any stretch of the imagination, but when she sang my heart melted. She sang of God's love with such conviction that I was overwhelmed by a mysterious and deep emotion. I didn't know it then but I was overcome by the power of what a Spirit-filled song could do to a hardened heart. My resolve not to trust God crumbled. In that one song my coat of self-reliance began to open up and something in me knew that I no longer had to fight things on my own and that I could call on him.

When she finished singing we listened to the evangelist, who spoke about the cross. He talked about Jesus and how he had come to take the sins of the world, my sins. He spoke of the trials that Jesus bore on the cross and how he suffered so that I no longer had to bear guilt or shame. I had heard that type of thing for most of my life but that day it finally became relevant and real. I understood that it was calling me to Jesus, the true friend and lover of my soul. The speaker then said something that captured my attention.

'There is someone here tonight who God has called before but you have not fully committed. He wants you to know that this is the last time he will ask you to surrender yourself to him. Three times he has called you, and this is the final call. Today is the day of your salvation.'

It was as though I was the only person in the room and the thousands of people around me had disappeared.

Before me was the cross and I could see myself kneeling down before it. As I did, Jesus reached out and with his hands scooped the torment I was feeling away from me. My history had been crushing me, but in that moment my mind cleared and the voices of the past that were taunting me day and night stopped. I was free and they couldn't hurt me again. As he finished preaching I knew what I wanted to do with my life. I had always wanted to sing, yes, but I wanted to sing like the girl in that very meeting had done. That day I gave God the final piece of me, my voice. I didn't want to fantasize and hide in song any more, but I wanted him to be the one I turned to.

Something inside me had yearned for God from the first call I had when I was 5 years old. He had tried to help me in the struggles that I had, even when I turned away. Things may not have gone well for me, but he *had* been there. He had given me on a Sunday the strength I needed for each week to endure the bullying. He had called me out at the gospel singer's concert and tried to save me from a path of destruction with the wrong kind of friends, and if I had trusted him instead of trying to impress the gang I would have steered clear of The Boy. I was 16 years old and God was there once again, calling me, and this time I decided to surrender completely to him and was determined to hold on to him no matter what the cost.

I became Sunday's child again and I rededicated my life to God. I always say that I was born again on Sunday 24 July 1988, even though I had a belief and faith before that time. It was the day I became God-conscious and not just God-believing. It was truly the day of my salvation and the point at which I placed my life in his hands. It was the day that I knew I belonged to him, he loved me and would never let me go.

8
Sunday's Child

Fathers, do not provoke your children, lest they become discouraged.

Colossians 3:21 (NKJV)

Even though the memories that tormented me were gone, and I sincerely wanted God to be all that I needed, I didn't understand that I was just at a middle junction of a very long journey. The past had let go of me but I had not let go of it, and remnants of old thought patterns remained. It was a hard struggle, and the traumas of my spring child-hood and summer teenage years had affected me severely. It was hard to trust anyone apart from God and I was still very guarded in my friendships. Angel and I would meet to pray and share music and faith, and I even started to make friends at church, but whilst I ensured I was friendly to all I never allowed anyone to occupy a place close to my heart.

I soon joined a house group and received a firm founda-tion in the basic doctrines of the Christian faith. By the time I was 17, which was four months into my recommit-ment, I became a helper at one of our church's branch Sunday schools. Although afraid to sing in public, I led wor-ship using just my voice and a tambourine. My favourite song was 'This is the Day' – it encouraged me to rejoice even though there were days that I didn't feel like it. I was a baby Christian in many ways, and I communicated with God by crying out in songs and poetry. It seemed the only way that I could truly convey what I wanted to tell him. My journal was little scraps of notepaper with scrawls and doodles of my thoughts and moods. Poetry became my outlet, songwriting was my release, and instead of singing being my life it became my prayer life. I sang constantly and every question, every doubt, I gave to God in song.

My career prospects started to improve and I was accepted into secretarial college to undertake a two-year apprenticeship.

Even though I wanted to be a singer, it was not going to be possible in the secular realm, and anyway I really wanted to sing gospel. When I sang to God all my nerves disappeared. I suppose it was because I was singing for a purpose and not just to win friends. I joined the evangelism team and every Saturday afternoon we would try to bring the gospel to Soho Road in Handsworth. It was a major step for me and a public declaration of my faith, as it was the very area that my former classmates and bullies were from. Sometimes I saw them walk by and laugh. I can't pretend it didn't bother me, as I was still somewhat scared of singing in public, but once I closed my eyes and opened my mouth to sing about the power of God's love something would flow through me. He was my confidence and strength and I found I was no longer afraid of them.

After a while I was invited to take part in an evangelistic crusade in Nigeria with my house group leaders and other members of the evangelism team. I couldn't believe that I would get to go to Africa and I was only 17 years old. At that time I was earning twenty-nine pounds per week as an office junior, which was a small fortune to me. Out of this income I would give some to my mother for housekeeping and the rest I saved for the ticket to Africa. Art, Indie and Mom gave me extra money for spending and even my father chipped in, though he wasn't too impressed that I was going. In fact he was quite negative about it, but I didn't mind. I was young and passionate in my newly awakened faith.

The trip proved to be the experience of a lifetime and I loved it. It was nerve-racking singing in Lagos and the surrounding areas at crusades to people in their thousands. I coped through prayer but also through food, and when it got too hard for me I would make myself vomit in order to cope with the stress of people looking at me. I did not know at the time that I had a disorder, as these things were not as widely talked about as they are now. All I knew was that was how I coped with stressful situations, and always had done. Because I had attended church most of my life others didn't see me as a 'baby' Christian, but as someone with a good grounding in the faith. I was very much a baby, however, and I had many lessons to learn. I was still in the process of change and God was changing one thing at a time. My eating habits still needed to be addressed, and the hot summer that I had endured was not yet over. I was about to go through a hurricane season that would shake me to the core and test my promise to trust in God.

Daddy's Girl

Before the time of Aunty B. my father had always seemed a very likeable man who captured my heart with his smile and deep resonating voice. At heart I was Daddy's Girl through and through, and when I was younger he'd take me out shopping, get my hair done and if he didn't like what I was wearing he would buy me something brand new. I didn't realize at the time that it was in a bid for one-upmanship over my mother. When I was young, a typical Sunday afternoon visit would involve him cooking Sunday lunch, which was superb and expensive, with fresh lobster and steaks the size of saucepans. After we had eaten we would play dominoes and card games and he'd laughingly try to get me to perfect my poker face. I really enjoyed his company back then, and as a young child one of my favourite things was resting my head on his large, round beer belly. But all these things changed.

By the time I was 15 the charm had disappeared, his drunken binges increased and I saw a more sinister side to his conduct. But although his parenting skills were practically non-existent, I was still his child and I knew no other daddy. He had never really been unkind to me when sober. Although, I have a habit of leaving my mouth open slightly when I'm concentrating – my daughter does it too, I think it's cute – and my father would snap at me, saying I looked dumb, and tell me to shut my mouth. That was as aggressive as he would get, but it was enough for me to know not to upset him. I believed it was alcohol that had changed him. Deep down inside my daddy was there, somewhere.

Although I feared and disliked him at times, I still loved him. He was the only dad I had.

After my disillusionment led me to renounce his name, however, he treated me like a servant. He wasn't physically abusive, but he wanted me to do his housework and that was all. He showed no affection, hugs or kind words, and he let me know that I had to earn his love and work for any money he gave me. A part of me didn't see why I should have to, although when I renewed my faith I tried to be a better daughter and help around his flat more, even cleaning up after his drunken binges. It was a vain attempt to turn the clock back to how it used to be. My father was not a believer but I was sure that he would be proud of the fact that I'd chosen to be a 'good church girl' and not go out and 'sow my wild oats'. I was wrong; my dedication to Christianity had the opposite effect. When I told him that I was getting baptized his response was curt and he told me bluntly what he thought.

'You're too stupid,' he said with disdain. From then on whatever tolerance he previously had for me completely disappeared.

One morning he called and said that he was sick and that he needed me to come and look after him. He could play the martyr very well, but I took his phone call seriously. He had fallen down the stairs before in a drunken stupor, so I got dressed quickly and took the half-hour journey on the bus to his flat. When I arrived I knocked on the door but there was no response, so I tried again. I tried repeatedly and when he didn't come to the door I worried that he had fallen and hurt himself. I shouted through the letterbox for nearly half an hour, fearing that he had suffered an injury but hoping that he had just gone out. Mobile phones were not around in those days, or if they were we certainly didn't have them, so I had no way of contacting him to find out where he was. In the end I went home in a state of worry. I told my siblings but wasn't sure what to do as I had no idea where he was.

Sometime later that afternoon the phone rang. It was him and I was relieved he was alright, but when I heard his voice I knew he was drunk. I told him I had been to his flat and he shouted down the phone that I hadn't, calling me a liar. Then he asked me how old I was, which I thought was a strange question so at first I didn't answer.

He asked me again, 'How old are you?'

'Seventeen,' I replied, and my answer seemed to trigger something inside him.

'Seventeen! Seventeen! And you don't know anyt'ing. Don't you know anyt'ing? Why are you so 'tupid and useless? You should know how to do things by now.'

He spewed out a vitriolic verbal attack and was not so drunk as to be incoherent. He answered each of his rhetorical questions with an insult. He told me that I was a waste of a daughter, a waste of a human being and that he wished I had never been born. I was, amid the expletives he used, useless, stubborn, stupid and he even said that he hated me.

The shock from this hit me like none other before. Even after all that had already happened to me I was not prepared for his words. Everything he said reverberated around not just my mind but my heart and whole body, and I shivered as I listened. I held the phone away from my ear with it welded to my hand as he shouted, but I could still hear every word. The first man in a girl's life – Daddy – was saying things that I had never thought I would hear him say. I had been called many vile names in the past but I could not believe that *he* was saying such ugly things to me. Other people had said them, but not him, not my father. Despite all his faults I still loved him and when I heard him say that he hated me I felt crushed. I knew what he was capable of, but I never thought that I would be the target of it. He ranted for so long that in the end I put the phone down on him – and then it hit me.

He said that I should know how to do things, but what things? I shuddered to think of what he wanted from me. I remembered the visits to the pub and didn't dare let my mind think about what my father might be referring to. A father is supposed to be someone who loves and protects his child, someone of whom the child can be proud. My father had exposed me to abuse, forced me to witness violence, sworn me to secrecy and had even paraded me as a girlfriend when I was just 15 years old. Yet still, he was the only father I knew and I wanted his love. His rejection was the single most catastrophic event that had happened in my life so far; above all the other things this hurt the most. I had been rejected plenty of times at school and had for many years felt insignificant. This event well and truly sealed my sense of worthlessness.

That afternoon my mother returned home from work to a broken-hearted daughter who couldn't stop crying. When I told her what happened she called him to 'give him what for' but when she finished I felt no better. She tried to comfort me by telling me not to worry, that he was always like that when drunk, and as soon as he sobered up I would see a penitent father, full of regret, remorse and apologies. This reassured me and I felt a little better thinking that he didn't mean the things he said and that it was just the booze talking.

By the time late evening came I retreated to the refuge of my bedroom and managed to calm down. I lay on my bed and closed my eyes, though I wasn't sleeping. I was disturbed by a loud knock at the front door. I could hear men's voices downstairs and went to the top of the staircase to 'assume the position', the one all children take when trying to eavesdrop, ready to run away as soon as detected. Kneeling like a sprinter, I tried to see who it was. When I did my heart sank. It was my father and he was blind drunk, with another man in tow. Arrogantly he demanded entry and that I come down to see him and he was led into the front room while I crept reluctantly and slowly downstairs. I was hoping that his impromptu visit meant that an apology might take place but I couldn't have been more wrong.

As I entered the room I said hello but he didn't speak. I walked to the other side of a small coffee table in the centre of the room. I stood beside my mother, opposite him; the smell of his pipe tobacco and the alcohol that oozed from his pores and breath filled the room. When he stood up I hoped he was going to apologize, even if drunkenly, but what followed was a further onslaught of abuse and attack. I wasn't surprised at his outburst, I had seen them before at other people, but I was surprised to be the victim. I said nothing. He was my father and I wouldn't dare argue back but that seemed to enrage him more, so he insulted me for being dumb and having that idiotic look on my face that he hated. At that he lunged at me across the table and I jumped back, trying to avoid the blows as his fists flew. My brothers Art and Indie, who had been standing by, stepped in and grabbed his arms to stop him from attacking me.

'If I ever see you again I will kill you, you hear me! You are not my daughter, and if I see you I will kill you.'

His eyes were bloodshot with alcohol but I knew his threat was real. What he said dug into my soul and severed whatever hope I had of reconciliation with him. My brothers forcibly removed him from the house along with his drinking buddy, who had sat watching in drunken amusement as if we had put on a soap opera for his entertainment.

In one evening I had gone from dismay to devastation; it felt as though a hurricane had swept through the core of my heart and ripped it out. I ran upstairs to my bedroom and screamed at God. As a recently recommitted Christian I had imagined that all the trauma of my childhood would not only be erased but also never repeated, and I couldn't understand how a loving God could let such a thing happen. Yet it had happened, and God was the only one I could turn to. In intense confusion I cried out in emotional agony as the pain hit me in waves. It was a tsunami of hurt in which I felt I would drown and never resurface.

The next day the apology my mother talked of did not come and days later when I plucked up the courage to call him, hoping he'd be sober, he wouldn't speak to me. As soon as he heard my voice he hung up the phone. He disowned me. For the next six months I lived in fear of my father. Afraid of seeing him, and believing his threat, I'd duck down in the Sunday school van whenever we drove past his home or shop.

I was desperate. I couldn't talk about it with anyone, the emotions were too raw. There was only one person I could talk to about how I felt, and one evening I knelt next to my bed, flicking through my Bible, searching for some kind of answer from God as to why it had happened. I was hurting again, but this time, instead of running away from God, I ran to him. I screamed, cried and pleaded with him for an answer. Why me? Why did bad things keep happening to me? Was I a bad person? What did I do wrong? Was I cursed? As I prayed I could see lying before me the coat of protection that was hate. Before my recommitment I would have hated my father, but I didn't want to do that again. I didn't want to react with hate, but I still felt it trying to cover me. I asked God to help me as I needed something to keep me on the path, and I turned to the account of Joseph in the book of Genesis (chapters 37–48).

The Joseph Connection and Rejection

Joseph was a boy who was somewhat spoilt by his father and had been encouraged, cherished and most of all loved. He was young and filled with both enthusiasm and folly, as are most teenagers. Joseph was not rejected by his father as I was, however, but by his brothers. I saw a parallel in our lives, as Joseph was half-brother to many, full brother to one. Being a half-sister to all my siblings, I understood how it felt to not be completely part of the family. The similarities began there, so I made it my aim to study the young man Joseph and see if there were any other connections. There are many men and women in the Bible who felt the same as I did, but there were few like Joseph; the story even speaks of him being the same age as I was, just 17 years old.

Although had heard the story in Sunday school, it was as if I had never read it before. Each day for weeks I studied Joseph and imagined myself in his shoes. I saw his story through my pain and wondered how he must have felt. He was the favoured child of his father, blissfully unaware of the intense jealousy of his siblings. I felt for him as he was rejected by his brothers. I cried for him, and with him. He had a dream and when he told his dream it infuriated his brothers to the point that they were intent on his murder, but instead they threw him into a pit and then sold him into slavery.

From being the favourite of his father he became a slave, someone else's possession. Joseph had never been away from the security of home, and his family was saying, 'We can do without you.' My father had practically said the same and it left me going round in emotional circles, crying when alone. I didn't know it, but I was grieving.

I knew how it felt to be despised so much that people no longer wanted you around. I had felt it nearly every day at school. Joseph must have had low points just like me. All my life I'd felt like I didn't fit in, and now as a Christian I was swimming against the tide of opinion. My dreams and desires ran contrary to everyone else's. I had dreams that my father deemed insignificant and called stupid. When I told him I wanted to be a gospel singer he laughed, saying that it would never happen. And it seemed he was right, as every door I knocked on got slammed in my face. His actions hurt so much that I could feel my old self wanting to resurface, but instead I buried myself in the Bible story and tried to make sense of it all. It seemed that God was showing me Joseph's heartbreaking experience in order to help me with mine.

When Joseph's family unit was torn from him he must have asked God questions, and with him I asked, 'Why me?' Joseph had been placed in a deep, dark pit, without any assurance of rescue or redemption. And when I found myself in my own pit, surrounded by thoughts of hopelessness, I knew I had to change my questions. Instead of asking why, I asked, 'Who will rescue me?' and 'When will it get better?' I knew Joseph's life changed dramatically later on, but it had taken years and I wanted mine put right immediately. Even though the story of Joseph showed that there was someone else who knew rejection and understood my pain, Joseph was different to me. He knew that his father loved him, and that love made him secure.

Being nurtured and loved brings security, and when these are taken away the mind can run rampant with doubt and mistrust. Not having love left me insecure, and that was the big difference between us. The Bible showed me that though I could understand Joseph's pain, I still didn't know the love that he knew. Joseph was assured of his father's love and I didn't have that. Yet, I could see that God was trying to encourage me to be secure in his love, to trust him. There were many lessons I learned from the biblical account of Joseph, and through them I grieved and gave the pain to God.

When his situation went from bad to worse and he ended up in prison, Joseph still had faith. I admired him greatly. Joseph could have chosen to give up hope, faith and his destiny, but something – Someone – kept him going. So I decided not to give up, but I also decided never to allow anyone close enough to hurt me like that again.

After being imprisoned for thirteen years, when finally he was released, a set of amazing circumstances led to Joseph becoming Prime Minister of Egypt. Pharaoh placed a ring on his finger and gave him new clothes and a new name. Was God telling me that he wanted to do the same for me: that I was to let him put *his* clothes on me; that I would wear the King's garments and bear *his* name? It was a great story, encouraging, inspiring and helpful, but that was all I allowed it to be – a story. I didn't think the happy ending would ever happen for me.

From the time Joseph's brothers sold him into slavery until he saw them again, twenty-two years had elapsed. Twenty-two years is a long time for a person to work through their emotions, and I have been just as long in working out mine. When the opportunity came and he was in a position to take revenge, he was tempted but didn't. He was not bitter, but ready to help his family in their time of need, and saw how God had worked in all things for the good of those who love him (Rom. 8:28). He forgave because he saw that God had taken a bad situation and turned it around.

Intellectually, I understood the message of forgiveness, and I could see that God was trying to get me to forgive, as Joseph had done, but the pain I felt overruled that particular lesson from the story. The story gave me comfort and inspiration, but that is *all* it did. The Joseph connection became the Joseph rejection as I rejected the message of forgiveness contained in the pages I read. But what I did at least understand from the account was that God was going to be there, even if the pit got deeper or darker. Joseph's story encouraged me to try to be secure in my heavenly Father's love just as Joseph had been. It also made me determined to try and make something out of my life. I was only 17, and felt that I'd had enough of what life had to offer, but I secretly hoped that I'd get a happy ending just as Joseph did.

9
Me, Myself, and I

The heart is deceitful above all things and beyond cure. Who can understand it?

Jeremiah 17:9

Not only had my relationship with my father been severed, but I soon found myself in a deteriorating family situation. Living at home became increasingly difficult. Looking back, I can see how my Christian convictions were seen as judgement by some of my siblings and, to be honest, there were occasions where I was a bit of a pious 'Pharisee'. I tried to block out love to the extent that it made me harsh and aggressive with my faith. I had a philosophy: if people didn't know my weaknesses then they couldn't abuse them, and if they didn't have my love they couldn't reject it. My love was a vulnerability that had been used by others, including family, as a weapon against me. As a result I believed that whatever I gave would only be thrown back in my face and I was not prepared to let that happen again. To my friends I was their confidante and provided counsel, but I never shared my own problems. It was my way of protecting my heart from pain.

The Bible talks about the heart being deceitful and I found it to be true because my own heart was cheating me.

I believed I could manage without love. I wanted love, but on my own terms, and I decided that God's love was enough – I could do without the love of others. But my philosophy was deeply flawed. God is love (see 1 John 4:8,16). His love cannot be bound or restricted by man's ideas of what love should be, and he was not going to allow me to restrict him either.

Against the Flow

As time went by I found it difficult to agree with some of my siblings on even the lightest of topics. It was hard being a Christian in a predominantly non-Christian household. We had all been brought up going to church but for many years, with the exception of my sister Pearl, my brothers and sisters had not attended and they were living other lifestyles. Even the smallest things caused conflict, like when I was asked to tell a tiny 'white lie', for example, and I refused. For me a lie was a lie with no grades or colours, but this was seen as being 'holier than thou'. It got so hard that in the end I became what they perceived me to be; I interpreted the Scriptures literally and lived by the law of the letters within. With teenage passion I saw the world as black and white, right and wrong, with no grey areas, and this led inevitably to confrontations and arguments. Although some of the things that happened were out of my control and I was not fully to blame for them, I can now see that my self-righteous behaviour at times got everyone's backs up. Christianity brings out extremes of feeling both for and against, and often divides families (see Matt. 10:34–36).

Within six months of my recommitment to the faith more members of the family weren't talking to me. Home started to feel like a battleground, but it felt like I was on the losing side and swimming against the tide. One confrontation, completely unrelated to my faith, even culminated in my brother Troy not speaking to me for nearly three years. I do not exaggerate when I say that he never said *one word* to me from the time I was 17 until I left home aged 20. The Bible's statement that a 'brother offended is harder to win than a strong city' (Prov. 18:19, NKJV) proved true, and no matter what the circumstance he would have nothing to do with me. If he came to visit and we were in the same room he would leave, as if my presence was repulsive. I was *persona non grata* for three dreadful years, and it caused such misery in me that I found it almost unbearable. It was the first and only time one of my family members had used the 'f' word when talking to me – and by that I mean *fat* – and it cut me to the core.

I tried to pursue forgiveness but it seemed useless when others held on to bitterness as a weapon against me. When others argued I turned the other cheek and did not respond with cruel words, and at each confrontation I chose silence as my defence. It was a true test of my faith and many times I wondered if the path was always going to be so hard. I even called my father at Christmas, on his birthday and on Father's Day to wish him well, and he listened to me talk but said nothing. It seemed like progress as at least he had stopped putting the phone down on me. I sent him cards, trying to reach out to him, but he never responded. Then, just before my eighteenth birthday he called me for the first time in a year. It was late at night and when I answered the phone I was drowsy, as I had been sleeping.

'Claudette, you be a good girl. I'm leaving now. Goodbye.'

I had heard rumours that he was going back to Jamaica but had never expected him to call me. It was a bizarre phone call that lasted for a few seconds. I said goodbye but didn't know what to make of it and went back to bed none the wiser. I later discovered that my father had called me just as he was about to board the plane. I also found out the reason why he suddenly upped sticks and went back to the West Indies. He had got an under-age girl pregnant and had to leave the country. He was in his early fifties at that point, and not only did the girl's father want to kill him but who knows what the authorities would have done if they had found out. I realize now that my father disowning me was probably one of the best things he ever did for me, as he was not a good influence. Finding out what he had done made me feel even more disgust for the man who was my father.

I couldn't talk to my family about it as my relationships with them were disintegrating and subsequent arguments even led me to spending my eighteenth birthday alone. At work, in my lunch break, I rang as many acquaintances as I could to try to get a place to stay since the situation at home was becoming so difficult. A couple that I knew from church agreed to put me up for a few nights, but after that I would have to make other arrangements. They had plans that evening, so they let me into the house and I was left alone. They had given me the only present I was to receive on the day of my eighteenth birthday, a box of chocolates. There was no food for me to eat, so I sat and ate the box of Ferrero Rocher for my evening meal. Unlike the well-known television adverts it was certainly no ambassador's reception or even a birthday celebration, and I remember going to bed not having received any cards and just that one present. It led to me loathing my birthday for years to come.

I went on from there to stay at my sister Pearl's house, which was just up the road from home. By that stage she was a busy mother with her own life, so I couldn't stay for long. Eventually, I managed to patch things up with some of my siblings, however, and went back home. My mother celebrated my birthday on my return, but in my heart it was too late. It was one hurt too far, and after I got home I lived out of my bags, not wanting to stay. I tried to find some-where else to live, but unable to afford to rent I had nowhere to go. I remember thinking during that time how it would be nice to have a proper father, someone to turn to, but I felt there was no one.

It is not necessary for me to go into too much detail about those years of my life as the issues are long forgiven by both my siblings and me. No blame is to be placed and no past dug up, but the reason I mention the difficulties is to show that I had become an expert at covering up how I felt. I didn't deal with my emotions or talk about them, I just buried them deeply. That was part of the process of toughening up – no one must see how much you are hurting. For years I tried to get so tough that I was like a fortress and wouldn't let anyone else in, yet there were periods where I crumbled and lost all my fight and the will to carry on. I have flipped from one state to the other. As a consequence, life revolved around me, myself and I.

One can only bury emotions for so long, however. If you keep on burying in the same spot, a mound, and then eventually a mountain of 'gunk' appears and symptoms begin to show. With some people it is bitterness or anger, but with me it was my old 'friend' bulimia. I was eating for comfort and not for pleasure, and I can't say that the food tasted sweet or had any redeeming qualities. Crucially, however, food didn't judge, disown, criticize and, most importantly, it didn't argue or fight. It didn't reject me or hate me – it was me who hated myself and I felt I should treat my body with the contempt that it deserved. Everyone else hated me (so I thought), and they must have had good reason. I felt I was to blame and that nothing good was ever going to happen to me. Pretty soon my weight ballooned to 14 st 10 lb (93.4 kg). Being then just under 5 ft tall (152 cm), this was a lot of weight for my tiny frame.

The Weight of Guilt

One day I was late for work and while running to catch the bus I fell and twisted my knee. Although it hurt I ignored the pain until after a couple of weeks, instead of getting better it had got worse. When the doctor examined it he told me that the knee would not heal because of the amount of excess weight I was carrying. The only way for it to recover was to ease the pressure the knee was under, so with the aid of the practice nurse I went on a healthy eating diet. I managed to lose four stone relatively quickly and it felt amazing. My knee healed I was now slimmer and I looked and felt great about my new-found figure.

However, soon enough I struggled with maintaining my weight, especially when a crisis occurred and I returned to bingeing. I believed that the only way that I could maintain the weight loss and binge eat for comfort was to increase the amount of times I forced myself to vomit. This behaviour continued through the first years of my Christian walk. I even went on evangelistic crusades and missions and all the while I was bulimic, but at the time I didn't know what I was doing as I hadn't even heard of the condition. The newspapers wrote about anorexia nervosa and on television people talked about that illness, and I knew I didn't have that. I honestly just thought that it was a way I could have my cake and eat it.

I held on to my faith and watched my relationships crumble around me. At odds with my siblings in lifestyle choices, I yearned for a friend. I had many friends but no special close friend, and I wanted someone in whom I could confide. There were times I almost shared things with my church friends, but any time I got close to doing so I would subconsciously (or maybe consciously) destroy the relationship with moody behaviour, or by deliberately pushing them away just to prove that they would not remain loyal. My policy was to reject others before they could reject me – not very Christian I know, but I knew no other coping strategy.

I would sit in church listening to people talk about things that were forever: eternity, everlasting life and love, but also friendship, brotherhood, sisterhood and more. I wondered if they were really 'forever'. I didn't doubt the doctrines of the Christian faith, or the foundations of my belief that included salvation, resurrection and eternal life – I was quite sure of those. What I struggled with was all the 'hidden extras' that came with it, such as the 'victorious life' I had to claim and the 'rights and privileges' that I was to proclaim. These sayings troubled me in my mindset as someone who had been the victim of bullying and abuse, suffered sexual assault and been disowned. The problem I found with these statements of faith is that they were just that – statements. For me they were not a reality, and the minute I didn't live up to the victorious life, or didn't say 'Praise God' to everything or rejoice in spite of the awful things that had happened to me, I felt a failure. It may not have been the intention of those who promoted that particular type of teaching, but sadly for someone suffering with an eating disorder, anything that remotely pertains to perfectionism is another millstone around one's neck.

There is a difference between what was said and what I heard. How I perceived these statements was that I should never be downcast and *always* have joy. Therefore I believed I was a failure because I was in sorrow over the loss of my father and the hurt of having a brother not speaking to me. We were told not to confess negative thoughts because it meant that you had 'cursed' yourself – a type of positive thinking that got me positively sinking. For someone like me, who was struggling to understand that 'there is now no condemnation for those who are in Christ Jesus' (Rom. 8:1), the practice of positive confession was difficult to follow. It sent me into a spiral of condemnation, as it led me to believe that my own negativity was to blame for everything that happened.

What I understood about salvation was that when I became a Christian all things were dealt with at the cross and I was made brand new by Jesus' sacrifice. I understood that I was granted eternal life that included relationship with Christ and forgiveness of sins. I acknowledged that the Bible said that God had healed me from the ordeals of the past and I believed that God loved me. *But no one could seem to tell me how to forgive or love myself.*

On the day I recommitted my life to God the torment stopped, but I still carried the weight of guilt and no one seemed to be talking about how to overcome that. I carried the guilt of my naivety for being abused, for being bullied and for being such a disappointment to my father. I couldn't love myself, as I believed I was ugly and unlovable.

Claudette aka 'Lame'

The meaning of the name Claudette is 'lame'. With this in the back of my mind, every time I heard that type of positive preaching I felt the curse of being called 'one who is lame'. I envied those who could claim a new name as a child of God, who could actually believe it and live accordingly. I wanted a new name like the one Joseph had been given when he eventually became a ruler in Egypt, but I had difficulty accepting the new name that God had chosen for me. It was a name that I felt was wrongly assigned and that I didn't deserve – that name was 'Beloved'.

A typical trait of an eating disorder is the feeling of inadequacy. I believed that no matter what I did I was never going to be good enough or 'make it'. So when I heard ministers speaking of walking in faith and victory it made me feel an utter failure, and I knew it couldn't be anyone else's fault but mine. I tried being the type of Christian they spoke of, but the ideal that they appeared to promote seemed unattainable for me. My thoughts were governed by my self-hatred and this distorted my understanding of the gospel message and what it truly meant. Yet all the while I yearned to be free from the habits of my youth; I struggled with my eating because I felt unloved. I struggled to accept that God loved me or believe that I was worth the sacrifice Jesus had made. I felt unloved by those around me, but perhaps worst of all, I was unloved by me.

I believed and loved God, yes, but by not loving myself enough to let him love me I was unable to walk in the victorious Christian life that I heard about. I had many lessons to learn on the journey to knowing that I am loved, and if I could have seen what God would do next I honestly would have run a mile, for a new season was coming.

Autumn was on its way. It happens to be my favourite of all the seasons. The leaves are stripped from the trees and they lay bare and naked in preparation for winter so that they can preserve and reserve their energy to reawaken in the spring. Just before the leaves drop nature looks at its most colourful and romantic. The leaves turn all shades of red, yellow and brown, and when they fall I love the crunch of them under my feet as I walk. Autumn signifies change, a change that illustrates warmth in its colours but belies the coldness of the winter to come. Little did I know that the change of autumn was to announce itself very forcefully indeed.

Autumn

Trust

Hurt parades,
Time fades,
Life evades,
Still . . . Trust.

Friends fail,
Pain impales,
Heart derails,
But . . . Trust.

Life bought,
Train thoughts,
Peace taught,
I . . . Trust.

10

The Leaves Are Turning

A friend loves at all times, and a brother is born for a time of adversity.

Proverbs 17:17

As a teenager I had tried to join the youth group at church, hoping to find people of similar age and experiences with like minds. Instead I found a place of exclusivity and cliques. No one really spoke to me, not even the youth leader, and after a couple of times of attending on my own, too shy to make friends, I gave up. So I stuck with the evangelism team as, although most of the team were a lot older, I enjoyed their company. I had been singing for the evangelism team for two years, but in our church street evangelism was not as highly regarded as other ministries and therefore neither was my singing ability. The focus was on the main meetings and on spiritual gifts and prophecy, but I didn't mind. I liked singing about Jesus to people on the streets. Street evangelism had a raw energy that spurred me on, although I was a nervous performer. I would close my eyes throughout each song and when I opened them I would be amazed to see that people had stopped in their tracks to listen, even when they had heavy shopping bags in their hands. They even used to come out of the pub opposite the spot where I used to sing, holding their beers and listening as I sang old hymns a cappella. Once the crowds drew near our team leader would zone in and grab them with a powerful message about the gospel, and other members would hand out literature to the onlookers.

My house group leaders, Amrik and Lorna Singh, headed up the evangelism team and they encouraged me greatly. They were the first ones to give me real opportunities to sing in public, and through them, under The Word Ministries, I took part in my first ever recording. We recorded a tape of the songs we did for evangelism and the simple music proved popular. The title song was a gospel chorus called 'Sign Me Up', a favourite of ours. I also sang the hymn 'The Old Rugged Cross'. Amrik and Lorna were passionate about Scripture and taking the gospel message to the streets. Doing street evangelism with them was a great training ground, and their belief in me had led to them taking me on evangelistic missions to Africa. Nevertheless, there were still times when rejection or humiliation seemed to be the order of the day.

Once, I was asked to sing in church, which was a huge honour as I had never been asked before. My reputation in the evangelism team as a singer seemed to be spreading, but I didn't know any pianists who would play for me and was too shy to ask. I was also not so sophisticated as to have backing tracks, so in the end I sang unaccompanied. I was 18 years old, and for the first time was standing on my own in front of a church full of people on a Sunday morning. I closed my eyes from beginning to end and held on to the pulpit for fear of fainting, as my nerves were that bad. As ever, though, I got lost in the words of the song and by the time I belted out the final chorus of the hymn my nerves had disappeared, although I still kept my eyes firmly shut. When I opened them everyone was applauding, apart from the leaders, who were sitting on the platform behind me. I hadn't even left the podium when the minister stood up sharply, came forward and snatched the microphone from me and told everyone to stop clapping. The congregation stopped in stunned silence. The minister said that the church only gave applause to children and that it was not appropriate in this instance. What he meant was that praise should go to God alone and not man, but the way he said it was humiliating. I held back the tears as I returned to my seat. From then on, whenever I sang I felt even more embarrassed to be in the limelight; being told that I did not deserve applause left an indelible mark on my spirit. It caused me to crawl further into myself, retreating emotionally once again.

A Friend at Last

In the two years since we had left school Angel and I remained good friends. After hearing how badly I had been treated, and knowing how much I loved to sing, she invited me to visit a choir she had joined. We were very different people from our schooldays, but we had two things in common – our faith and a love of gospel music – so I agreed to attend one of the practices with her. The group was formerly a mass church choir that had recorded an album and had a great reputation, but its glory days were long past when I visited. Issues to which I was never made privy had reduced it to a tiny independent choir, with less than twelve members. However, what they lacked in numbers they made up for in the quality of the remaining members, as it was a true old-time gospel choir with big voices and even bigger personalities. I was nervous in new company but I enjoyed the rehearsal, so when Angel invited me to one of their prayer meetings taking place later on in the week, I agreed.

It was at the house of a divorced, single mum called Sista. She was in her late thirties and was a woman with a huge personality and a heart to match. I had never met anyone like her before in my life; Sista was quite a sight to behold. Dressed in an aqua-green shell suit with curly permed hair she somehow managed to look extremely glamorous. By the time Angel and I arrived the other people were already settled in, quite relaxed and chatting freely, but I sat down quickly in the corner of the room, partly in fear of this larger than life character. She seemed very theatrical, and I had certainly had enough of drama, so I kept a low profile and tried to make sure there was a good distance between us in the small living room. Even though the house was warm and inviting, I sat down as if I were frozen. Determined to try to make myself invisible, I didn't want anyone to notice me, especially her, and was truly relieved when we got on with the purpose of the meeting.

We started to pray but my mind was searching for answers on what direction to take in my life. I silently prayed and asked God for a friend, just as I had done when I was a child. I was tired of being lonely and I needed to be able to confide in someone about my eating. Every time I binged and purged I felt that there was something not quite right about it, and it weighed heavily on my conscience. It was an issue for prayer, but for me only, up till now, as I had been too ashamed to share it with anyone else.

We had been singing and praying for around half an hour when suddenly Sista, who was on her knees, shot bolt upright and pointed at me. 'You, upstairs now!' she said loudly, and I looked around the room in the hope that she was pointing at someone else, but instead found everybody looking at me. To say I was scared was an understatement. I hardly knew the woman — what on earth could she want with me? Backed into a corner in front of virtual strangers, there was little I could do but comply, as she didn't look like the kind of woman I could refuse. She led the way and I followed her upstairs to her bedroom where she nodded for me to sit down, and in dread I sat tentatively on her bed. Sitting down next to me she then said the most amazing thing.

'God has told me to be your friend. He said that you have never had a friend and he wants me to be there for you.'

In utter disbelief I gawped at her and I shook my head, thinking that it was sheer madness. She looked sincere. But how did she know I had never had a proper friend, even though I had come to the meeting with Angel? Was

God really telling her? Pentecostal Christians are very charismatic, and like to operate in spiritual gifts such as prophecy, but I was still very wary of that type of thing. I remembered when the gospel singer had spoken and called out the bullied child. I had gone forward, but my life did not improve after that – far from it, in fact, it got worse. How could I be sure that it wasn't going to happen again? Could I trust her? Was she for real? She sat opposite me and didn't say anything as I examined her face. She looked kind enough, but I shook my head again and finally decided not to trust her. I determined to put on my tough survival coat and gave her one of my looks. If you have ever seen a vexed black woman then you know that it was a fierce look, and those who know me will know the look. At that, the gauntlet was laid down and the battle began, and in the next moment she grabbed me.

'God has told me to give you a hug like you've never had before,' she said, and with that her arms went around my shoulders and she pulled me towards her so violently that I was sure she'd broken my ribs. I wanted to pull away and get out of the room and her house, convinced she was insane. As she held me close I struggled, but soon I felt tears falling down my face. Before I knew it, I stopped struggling and a gut-wrenching howl came out of me that seemed to last forever. I held on to her and cried like a baby. It was the most vulnerable I had let myself be in front of anyone for years, and afterwards I was completely drained. For a long while Sista held me in her arms, cradling me like a child. I wasn't sure if I could trust her, but I remembered that I had asked God for a friend, a confidante, and she seemed to be the one that he was sending. Thus, the friendship began.

It was an unlikely match because Sista was an effervescent, enchanting, confident woman with a big laugh, and I was shy – painfully so. She seemed to ooze self-assurance out of every pore and loved people and company. I was the complete opposite, lacking self-belief and shying away from anything that focused attention on me. I could not get to grips with the fact that this woman wanted to get to know me because God told her to, and that she was going to obey. God seemed to know best, as she had bucketloads of personality and I had none, or so I thought. Initially our friendship was a rocky one, as I fought her all the way; I wasn't sure I could trust her. However, she proved herself to me in my first minor emotional crisis after that meeting.

My family had won a competition to have our pictures taken professionally and everyone attended with all their spouses and children. By that time the family was quite large and our mother even invited my siblings' father along so that there could be one big family portrait. I have to admit that I felt a bit odd at that, as he wasn't *my* dad, but in the end they were my family so I went along anyway. Troy was still not speaking to me and I was barely getting on with my sisters, so the photo shoot was difficult, for me anyway, but I still had my picture taken. First, the whole family had a portrait and then different branches of the family had theirs done: Indie and his family, Troy and his family, and Pearl and her family all took turns. Then we had one with just the brothers and then the sisters. Soon it was just the kids left, the youngest three. I went to join my two sisters, Special and Serene, when Special said, 'No, not you, just Serene and me.' I know now that she didn't mean to hurt me; we had grown apart and they were naturally closer to each other. However, at the time I saw this as one more rejection: once again, someone didn't want me.

Afterwards I was upset, and was about to revert to my usual method of internalizing my problems and comforting myself with food, when I decided to go and visit Sista instead. It always took her a while to get me to talk about anything troubling me, so we ate dinner, watched television, and when her young daughter went to bed I eventually told her about my day. She offered me a place to stay, away from it all, and it meant a lot to me that she was prepared to put me up for the night. After that I became a semi-permanent house guest with Sista, and she and her daughter were like family to me. After a while I finally told her about my eating and she began to help me. She was the first person to refer to what I was doing as bulimia and she tried to explain to me about that type of eating disorder. She was a great support when I was in need and although trusting her was new and frightening, it was good. I had a friend at last. She tolerated and forgave my moods and through my friendship with her, from the age of 18 until I was 20, I finally learned to trust someone as a friend and not to expect betrayal, bullying or rejection. I grew to love her deeply.

Womanism

The best way to describe the type of thought process that I had when I was with Sista would be to use the terms sisterhood or 'womanism'. (Although I didn't know it at the time, the term 'womanism' would come to be used to describe a form of feminist thought to acknowledge black women's natural contribution to society in distinction to the association of feminism with white women. I hasten to add that this was not what Sista called it, nor am I intending to embark on a critique of the feminist movement, but it is the way that I interpreted the things I was told and this was simply the term that came to me to describe my experience.) Sista lived a kind of Christian feminism, believing in the empowerment of women and that we could do what the men could not, or would not, do.

My view on men, whom I didn't particularly like, sat well with the kind of positive thinking that Sista encouraged me to pursue. These beliefs were not written, literal ones, but 'womanism' was the prism through which I came to interpret life, the Bible and my friendship with her. To sum it up, I became a woman who did not need a man and thought perhaps women were better than men. Good men were in short supply, and there were quite a few negative examples for me to believe myself better than. This philosophy worked well for anyone who had ever been downtrodden or hurt by men, and I'd had my fair share of that. I found my voice in the confidence this instilled in me. However, years later, when speaking to my mother about that time in my life, she said that I had come across as a bit aggressive and quite judgemental.

This was my new way of toughening up without hating or fighting, and I grasped these new garments of self-reliance and independence. It was what I needed at the time, as on the measuring scale of confidence I was -100. 'Womanism' was an antidote to many years of negativity. This philosophy of positive confession led to a somewhat simplistic and judgemental view of the faith, one in which there was only right or wrong, black or white, my way or the highway. Passion and the young go hand in hand, and I embraced this 'womanism' in its entirety. Crucially, through it I stopped the bulimic behaviour that had troubled me: I was no longer bingeing and purging.

Time of Change

In the four years that had passed since my schooldays I had trained as a secretary and, although I didn't really enjoy office work, I found that I was very good at it. I passed my secretarial exams and got qualifications in typing and business administration, but at the end of it all I felt frustrated. Going to Nigeria with the evangelism team had given me a taste of a different world and a yearning for a new life. So I left my permanent job and became a temporary worker, flitting from one job to the next. I found it suited me, as it meant I didn't need to forge lasting friendships. I let one person close – Sista or 'Sis' as I used to call her – but no one else. I still had mood swings off which you could ring a bell, and my past was still affecting me. I didn't know my life plan or purpose, but I did know what I wanted.

I wanted to be away from home, I wanted to study and I wanted change. The life of a secretary was not for me. I was thirsty for knowledge, although what I really needed was 'understanding' (Prov. 4:5). I studied the Bible voraciously, trying to understand it and, more importantly, apply it, but failed miserably. I didn't know it but the leaves were turning and change had begun. After going to Africa on a mission for a second time, I made the decision to give up work and go to Bible college in order to learn more about the faith that I sang about.

It was a crazy notion for someone like me, with the bare minimum of academic qualifications. No one in my immediate family had been to university or even lived outside a two-mile radius of the family home. I was proposing to do both, and though I was scared of what the future would bring there was one thing I had finally learned to do, and that was to trust God concerning my future and not to try to force change myself. I had learned from the mistakes of my youth, and though I wasn't sure I would even be accepted, in early 1992 I applied to go to an Assemblies of God Bible college called Mattersey Hall.

Along the way I met opposition. I had little support from my minister and in order to get a reference my house group leader had to go in to bat for me. He asked her, 'What does she want to go to Bible college for? She's already got a ministry.' To which Lorna replied, 'Then why didn't you acknowledge her?' And even when my application was accepted, I still didn't have my first term's fees, which was a prerequisite for attendance. Although some members of the church had said that they would sponsor me, I still lacked the thousand or so pounds that were needed. I committed myself to prayer, as there was no way I could raise the money, and even a week before I was due to start I still had insufficient funds. There was no government funding for the course I wanted to do, so my mother approached our local councillor, who was also a Christian, but she wasn't able to help.

It was difficult, but I chose to wait on God for a miracle. Whilst I believed by faith that God would supply my needs, as promised in Philippians 4:19, it was hard to convince others; at one point I was called lazy and stubborn because I wasn't considered proactive enough in getting the money. It is hard to have faith, dreams and desires and even harder for others to see them in the same way. Amidst increasing opposition, at times even I began to doubt and I rang the college to tell them that I could not attend. I was put through to the principal, who asked which church I came from. When I told him he said he was surprised that I wasn't being funded by the church, as it had a great reputation for supporting aspiring missionaries and Bible college students. He then said, 'Just leave it with me.'

The next day I had a phone call from one of the trustees of the church, Doreen. She was also the leader of the Sunday school at which I had been teaching and leading worship for three years. She was the first person who had encouraged me to go to Bible college after she saw how much interest I had in the Bible. She rang to tell me that the church was going to take a collection the following Sunday and I would have my first term's fees. It wasn't the way I expected it to happen, but the money came through and three days before I was due to go I not only had my first term's fees but enough money for my keep as well.

Doreen told me that the principal had called my minister personally, asking whether anything could be done, and as a result he reconsidered his decision.

That Sunday I was asked to sing and this time the minister allowed the members to applaud. I was overwhelmed by the amount of support I was given, and it was the first of many times that I would see God changing man's rejection into acceptance. It taught me to trust God to fight my battles. Frequently I had felt bypassed by the ministers. However, I now saw that God was my vindicator and my advocate (see Ps. 135:14; Job 16:19). I didn't have to fight things on my own.

The Unforgiven

Just a few weeks before leaving home to travel to a new life at college, I had one final encounter with my father. He had been away for two years and had come back to England for a two-week visit to settle his business and finally sell up. I had no idea he was in the country, so it was a shock to come home from work one day to see him sitting in the kitchen, pipe in hand, wearing his camel coat and trilby hat. His impromptu visit was as unwelcome as it was unannounced, and I hoped the fact that he had kept his coat on was a sign that he was about to leave. He had not changed very much, but I had. I was pleased that he no longer frightened me, but another emotion soon came to the fore. I was stunned by the amount of hurt I still felt; I could only be polite and say hello, but nothing else. He didn't remark on how I had grown or changed, and made no effort to communicate with me directly. When my mother told him I was going away to study theology, she might as well have said that I was becoming a nun, as he sneered and curled his lip, as if the very mention of anything to do with God was repugnant. I wanted to leave the room but from the look on my mother's face I knew I had to stay. So I watched in silent suspicion, wondering why he had come if he wasn't even going to speak to me.

Bizarrely, he had brought some meat with him and he ordered me to cook it. It seems odd to me now, but that is what I did, and for the next half hour he watched me whilst I cooked and he talked to my mother. When I finished cooking I served it to him and watched him eat, and with every chew of his mouth my hurt increased. Once again he was trying to put me in my place as servant and not daughter, showing he had not changed. Like so many others he could not offer me an apology and, remembering the days when he forced me to go to the pub with him, I inwardly dared him to try to offer me money. I wanted the pleasure of throwing it back in his face, but he didn't. Unrepentant and arrogant, he made me feel he didn't deserve my forgiveness. When he left I nodded my goodbye but had nothing to say to him. I was nothing to him, and I wanted him to become nothing to me.

The next day it was Sista's birthday so I went to see her and I told her about my unwelcome visitor. We shared a slice of cake that I had made for her, a Victoria sandwich with strawberries and cream, even though I never usually ate strawberries as I didn't like them. I shared my troubles and later that evening I travelled home, but within a few hours fell ill. My fingers began to swell then all my joints became swollen. My mother called the doctor, who said that I must have had a reaction to the strawberries since they were the only new thing in my diet, and she gave me a shot of antihistamine. Believing it would calm down I went to bed, but awoke in the early hours with an aching body and when I tried to sit up I was struggling to breathe. When I finally managed to get up I looked in the mirror and what I saw was mortifying. My eyes, lips, cheeks, the whole of my face, in fact, was horribly swollen and disfigured. I turned to my mother and shook her awake. She jumped with shock at the sight of me and called the emergency services.

They took me to hospital and the medical staff said that I had come just in time, because given my breathing difficulties I could have died. At this my mother called my father to tell him what had happened. He had been in our house the day before and although we had not spoken I wondered if his unexpected visit was a sign that he possibly wanted to see me, even if he didn't want to talk to me. But he seemed to want to exact some kind of revenge. He flatly refused to come. She reiterated how ill I was, and that I could have died, but he still wouldn't come. This was the final rejection – and it hurt. I knew that I hadn't been overly welcoming when he visited, but I had been polite and courteous and had even cooked his meat for him. I wondered why he couldn't just swallow his pride and at least pretend to care. I had not forgiven him because he was unrepentant, and now, when I wanted him to care, he would not forgive me. The cycle of retribution was complete.

I spent a week in hospital and by the time I was discharged he had returned to Jamaica. I resigned myself to the fact that we were never to meet again. The only bonus for me was that I had lost even more weight and was now technically slim. I say technically, as I was a recovering bulimic and as such never felt I was slim enough. After undergoing numerous tests the hospital couldn't pinpoint exactly what had happened to me and I was told I'd either had an allergic reaction or a polyarthritis virus, and I was severely anaemic. Either way, I was told to stay away from strawberries and to look after my health. I did the former, but not the latter, and prepared for a new life at college.

Before I knew it I was ready to go. In late September 1992 my brothers Art and Indie and my mother drove me and all my belongings to college. It was over a hundred miles away from home, which doesn't seem a great distance now, but for an inner-city girl whose life revolved around a council estate it was like moving to the other side of the world. Set in a remote village in the picturesque countryside of South Yorkshire. Mattersey Hall would be my home for the next three years. I didn't know what the future held but it didn't matter, as I was finally leaving behind Birmingham along with all the memories it contained. With the support of my new friend, Sista, I was finally happy. I had been an office worker for four years and it hadn't given me enough money to get a place of my own; at the age of 20 I was embarrassed to say that I was still sharing a bedroom with my mother. At last I would have my own private room with space to think.

I was ready to embrace life as a student and I saw it as a fresh start, with no school bullies, no drunken father, no family feuds and no history. I thought I could begin anew, but I thought wrong. I had left behind the place that reminded me of my past – but the past came with me.

11
The Fatherhood
of God

A father to the fatherless, a defender of widows, is God in his holy dwelling.

Psalm 68:5

At first living at Mattersey Hall wasn't the supreme adventure that I thought it was going to be. We lived in what I jokingly called a 'goldfish bowl'; it seemed like the original *Big Brother*. We lived in halls of residence with no television but a list of rules that felt like restrictive legal statutes. This was a great disappointment for someone like me who wanted to break free. I had my own room but little privacy as the walls were paper-thin. We also had communal dining, which was a nightmare for a recovering bulimic. It was akin to boarding school and, as I had never lived away from home before, I was dreadfully homesick. I yearned for the familiar as I tried to adjust to being with some of the strangest Christians I had ever met.

After becoming a Christian I had decided to avoid secular music, as I knew how highly I cherished it. I didn't go to the cinema, drink alcohol, or participate in what I would then have called 'worldly' pursuits. In fact, some of the restrictions I placed on myself were rather ridiculous. The

Christians I met came from all walks of life, imposing different conditions on themselves and consequently on others. Some listened to pop music, some didn't; some frequented pubs, and I certainly didn't. Some were still dealing with habits such as smoking, which was more visible than the bulimia I dealt with inwardly. I was therefore unfairly judgemental of some of my fellow students' behaviour. I saw them as dissolute – drinking, smoking and indulging in other worldly pursuits.

On the other side, there were the spiritual extremists – Bible-bashing fundamentalists, who, to be honest, scared me just as much as the 'worldly' bunch. It took a while for me to settle in and finally make friends with a set of 'normal Christians' (although I think that term itself is a bit of an oxymoron, as there is nothing normal about Christianity, or my friends!). Amongst the friends I made were two people who are still dear to me: Calvin Allcoat, a cuddly bear of a man, whose heart of compassion knows no ends, who now pastors a church in Northern Ireland; and Sandie Tutty, a girl from Ireland who went on to become a Bible college lecturer. Sandie's calm, collected ways were the perfect antidote for my erratic behaviour and Calvin's wise, brotherly heart always gave the right advice, even if at times I didn't want to hear it. These were and are special people, who helped me on the way to finding the love that God had waiting for me. Together we had many lessons in the classroom, although Mattersey was not just about studying, it was also about acquiring life skills for Christian ministry. I learned a lot in the lectures but one of my main lessons was outside of the classroom, and it began with an 'essay' in jealousy.

Watching

As part of our training, the college sent the students out on placements on Sundays to different churches, to assist the pastor and hopefully get to preach every now and then. I did not want to preach so I sang, which at the time is what I thought I did best. My first placement was at a church in Doncaster and, being there the whole day, we would have to go to people's houses for Sunday lunch. Members would take turns to host the students, and one week the group I was with went to the home of a West Indian couple, Fred and May. I latched on to May straight away because she reminded me of my mother, whom I missed, and before long I spent more time with the couple, even staying the odd weekend as well. At college it was a struggle living with so many strangers, each with their own 'baggage' and perspectives on God and the universe, and a night at Fred and May's was a dose of normality and home.

Fred was a quiet man, but as I watched him with his family I saw an honourable commitment that was unwavering. It was upsetting when a few months later he passed away. When May asked me to sing at his funeral I felt such sorrow that they had lost a man who was so committed to his family. As I watched his children I could see that they loved him. If it were my father that had died, I couldn't say I would feel the same. I had not had the example of a good father in my childhood and until then I truly believed that a father was a worthless waste of space who I could well do without. Upon meeting Fred I started to see what a good father was like. And, I have to say, it hurt to see what I had missed. I didn't know that in reality I was yearning for the Father's love.

Learning

In the summertime between my first and second year at Mattersey I worked on-staff in order to help pay for my fees. This involved cleaning, and lots of it, waitressing and any other work we were called on to do. There were quite a few of us working under the supervision of the maintenance engineer, an ex-miner called Johnnie Bradwell, and his wife, Enid. They were true northern folk. Straight talking but friendly, they were salt-of-the-earth Christians and as I worked in the college during that summer I got to know them. I had never met anyone like them before, or since, and the love they showed me still influences me to this day. I learned valuable lessons from the couple, and Enid was a loving mother-figure who befriended many of the students. As the months went by I spent more time in their company and when the college term resumed I would visit their house. I was amazed that I even felt comfortable enough to sit next to Johnnie without fear. I allowed him to hug me, which was a miracle – I didn't 'do contact', as I often told people back then. My childhood experiences meant that I didn't allow anyone, especially men, to touch me. But during my time at college, through the friendships I had made I gradually came to change my negative feelings about men.

Seeing a functioning, loving marriage up close for the first time was a marvel. Coming from a single-parent family, I hadn't seen first-hand any examples of good husbands or a fathers – watching them was a real education. I wasn't sure if I dared to hope that one day I could be married with a family of my own. It seemed too fantastical an idea, and it was the first time that I had allowed myself to dream or imagine such a thing. Nevertheless, envy would surface when it came to the issue of fathers. As much as I knew that Johnnie and Enid cared for me, I wasn't their daughter and they had their own children, whom I had no desire to replace. My jealousy was one of not understanding why I couldn't have had a childhood like theirs instead of the one I had endured. I felt angry that I had a waster of a father who didn't care for me, and I felt the pain of what I'd missed. The glimpses of what a father should be filled me with sadness. Each time I saw these good men with their own children, jealousy would raise its ugly head. As I watched father with daughter, laughing and scolding each other in jest, I questioned God; it felt unfair that I should be fatherless. They seemed to have their father to turn to in times of trouble, but I had no one. I had my mother, yes, but I hated to burden her with the struggles of my life when she had so many of her own. At that time I couldn't see that God was showing me these people to demonstrate how he wanted to be a Father to me; it was a lesson of love but I had a very long way to go.

Hurting

This type of jealousy was new to me. I had never encountered anything like this before. I had always felt the hurt of my father's rejection but I had not known what a father should be like or what I was missing, until now. One Sunday morning, however, whilst at my church placement, as the worship band went through their set list of songs, I could think about little else. It was only when the band played the song 'Father God I Wonder' that I realized what I was truly missing:

> Father God I wonder how I managed to exist
> Without the knowledge of your parenthood and your loving care.
>
> *Extract taken from the song 'Father God I Wonder' by Ian Smale,*
> *© 1984 Thankyou Music*

The congregation began to sing but something about the words arrested me and I couldn't join in. I had sung the song many times before; it spoke of praise and I understood that. I understood thanking the Lord for what he had done in saving me from sin, hell, death and my own self-destruction, but the first lines I had always sung as a matter of course, never really thinking of God as my Father. That particular morning, the words struck me as never before. I really didn't know his parenthood or his loving care.

I didn't know him as Father.

I opened my mouth to try to sing the song but I couldn't get past the words 'Father God', so I sat down, not understanding why I couldn't sing the song. Every time I tried to say 'Father' a realization of love unravelled the meaning of the word to my heart and I found it overwhelming. I tried to fight the feeling and was terrified of the sensation that was invading my very being. God was my Father. But fathers hurt you, let you down, disown you – and I couldn't accept that God was that person. The only father I had known was negative, judgemental and condemning. God wanted to reveal himself as the perfect Father to me, however, and had shown me Fred, Johnnie and other examples in order to help change my distorted perspective. Even though I now wanted to know God as Father, I really didn't know how I could.

When I got back to college I thought about it through the night. Knowing God as Father meant opening up my heart to love, and I wasn't sure I was capable of doing that. I had received the gift of salvation and thought that was all I needed in order to live a Christian life, but God wanted me to accept more – I needed love. Whilst at college I saw many well-adjusted children have no difficulty in receiving presents from their fathers – from fathers who gave without expect-ation, or any motive other than to make their children happy. The children didn't have the false humility or pride of adults – they opened their gifts eagerly, with their faces shining in delight when they got what they wanted. I watched them shout with glee, say a quick 'Thank you' and run away to play with their new gift. They never said, 'I don't deserve it' or 'I can't accept that'. There was no feeling of self-depreciation or unworthiness in their minds. All they knew was that their fathers had bought them a present and it was theirs to have and to own forever. No questions, no doubts.

I hadn't acted like the children I had seen towards God. It's true that I had received the baptism of the Holy Spirit about a year after salvation. I could accept that, easily. Spiritual gifts and power was what my supposed philosophy of 'womanism' was about – but love? All-consuming, unconditional love? No way! I was like a child on their birthday who saw all their wrapped presents but decided to open all the small gifts and never open the biggest, best and most important present of all. No child would do that, but that is exactly what I had done when it came to God's love. I wanted everything else he had to offer, but his love seemed too much. This revelation was powerful and overwhelming, and it frightened me. Although Jesus said that we were to receive the kingdom of God as a little child (Mark 10:15), I remember thinking about how difficult that would be for someone like me. The vulnerable, open, trusting little child that I envisaged receiving God's kingdom was nothing like the young woman I had become.

Spoilt Children

I spent that night arguing with God and told him that the pain that I had experienced was part of my history. He showed me that I was letting it be part of my future also. I responded that I had gone through the tough time, no one else – it was mine, and it made me who I was, and I wasn't going to let go of it. It sounds crazy that I would hold on to my past, but the truth is I had got used to it and on the other side was now the terrifying unknown. Embracing the Fatherhood of God meant throwing away all my preconceived ideas about who I thought he was. It meant embracing love, vulnerability and forgiveness, things that to me epitomized weakness and sensitivity, two character traits I had tried to run away from since my childhood.

Some children can be spoilt, petulant, ungrateful and downright obnoxious, and whilst I would like to think that I wasn't any of the aforementioned, I have to admit that I can be headstrong and I know I had, and still have, traces of some of these running through my personality. So, although I had come to an epiphany of sorts and started to understand that God was my Father, I persisted in resisting his love. God, however, continued to teach me this lesson all through my years at college, and it was painful. Painful because I was determined not to let go of the pain my earthly father had caused me. The one thing about the Father heart of God, however, is that a true father never gives up on his child. And God wouldn't give up on me. Therefore, he persisted with me until I accepted his love. My understanding of his heart was limited and I still didn't fully comprehend the true depth of his love. But instead of beating me into submission with chastisement or rebuke, he tenderly brought along a love that would not only further demonstrate to me how much he cared but would finally strip away the remaining coats of my past.

12
A Love Too Far

To love another person is to see the face of God.

Victor Hugo, *Les Misérables*

Before becoming a Christian I had decided that men were strictly out of bounds and even though I'd had a couple of crushes I had never let them get beyond that. The events of my past had scarred me sufficiently to make me very wary of any man that paid an interest in me, not that any did. However, after spending time with Johnnie and Enid and seeing how great their marriage was, I found myself thinking about relationships. At 22 years of age I started to think about the prospect of a future of spinsterhood. My friend Sandie and I became inseparable whilst at college and we shared our woes on being singletons in a place where everyone else seemed to be pairing up. Calvin would give us moral support (he was already taken and was engaged to be married) but campus soon seemed like 'bridal college' rather than Bible college.

I was in the latter half of my second year and had fully embraced college life. I still had erratic moods that obviously had a root cause, but my friends could never find out why. It was too painful to talk about my father or events from school. Then one day Calvin handed me a note. Although he was nervous about giving it to me he was obedient to what he felt God had told him to do. I was in an apathetic mood and had still not accepted fully the message of love and forgiveness that God was trying to teach me. I had so many questions and couldn't understand why life had been so cruel and painful. Calvin's note was exactly the kick up the backside that I needed:

The vision will be fulfilled, but as I told you before my priority is you, not your work. At present I AM rebuilding your walls, but there is rubble which first must be swept away. Now I AM showing you what the rubble is, why it came to be, and how it is to be removed, so be patient with yourself and be patient with me.

Some of the rubble is bits and pieces of an earlier 'you' which was truly good, but was destroyed when the enemy took advantage of your youth. I AM making all things new. But the sooner the old ruins are removed the sooner the new 'you' will emerge. Therefore work in joy and work in hope! I AM with you.

The strength you need is within 'you'. I know this because it's I AM who put that strength within, draw upon it and allow me; I will rebuild, reshape your walls. I hear your questions, 'Why?' You now have to listen to my answers. Be open and allow me to work through you. I LOVE YOU and have always promised that I will NEVER LEAVE you, trust me!

Word via Calvin Allcoat, 9 March 1994

Apart from Sista, I had never shared details of my past life with even my closest of friends, so when I read the note it blew me away. God used Calvin to write me a love note of such poignancy, that when I received this message I determined to try to allow God to sweep away the ruins of the past. I prayed for God to help me to let go, and I gave him leave to do whatever he wanted to do.

Those were unbelievably brave words from someone who didn't really know what they were saying. Be aware that when you tell God that he can do whatever it takes to get you sorted, guess what? . . . He will.

Won't Someone Just Like Me?

The first change in me I noticed was a yearning for a boyfriend. Up till now I had determined that I neither needed nor liked men. I had always blocked out any thoughts of liking someone but soon after Calvin's note I felt the loneliness of my existence. I had friends, but when I saw the abundance of couples on campus I felt a sense of missing out. One evening I called Sista to have a good moan about it. She had become my sounding board. These were the days before mobile phones had become an essential accessory, so I walked to a payphone outside campus for privacy and had a good old Brummie 'whinge' to her. I just wanted someone to ask me out so that I'd know I was a little bit attractive. I would say no, of course, as all I really wanted was for someone to show a bit of interest in me. I asked Sista if I was ugly, as no one had even so much as smiled or winked an interest in me, and she laughed, giving me as much encouragement as she could. I went back to the halls of residence feeling a bit better and knowing that I too would probably laugh it off the next day.

The next day I wasn't laughing. I still felt lonely. I attended lectures as usual and after lunch went to do my duties, as we all had manual tasks to undertake on a rota basis. I wore my Walkman and listened to music as I vacuumed the dining hall and, as usual, tried to sing away my troubles. A first-year student that I knew as an acquaintance came up to me and tapped me on the shoulder. I jumped, startled, as I had been unaware of him standing behind me.

'Oh, hi Michael, how are you?' I said as I switched off my headphones.

'OK,' he said quietly. He stood there for a minute blushing slightly, but said nothing more. An uncomfortable silence followed and I shrugged my shoulders. I wondered if he wanted anything, or if I had missed a spot whilst I was cleaning. Still he stood in front of me and stared but said nothing. I was about to turn my Walkman back on when finally he spoke and asked me if I would go for a walk with him.

'I want to talk to you about something,' he said earnestly.

I nodded and arranged to meet him in the dining room at six o'clock after the evening meal. He disappeared as suddenly as he had popped up, and when he was gone I continued cleaning. Instead of listening to music I thought about the strange conversation I'd just had, and was flummoxed as to what he could possibly want to talk to me about. He was a mere acquaintance, a foreign first-year student whom I had first encountered when he had been at college for just a few days. We had been in the kitchen on washing-up duty. Because I was a second-year student I was the team leader, so I had introduced myself to the 'freshers' on my washing-up team and Michael was one of them. I remember telling him my name and him getting it completely wrong.

'Closet?' he laughed. 'That is a *toilet* in my country.'

I rolled my eyes, smiled sarcastically and told him my name a second time, enunciating every vowel and consonant, speaking louder and slower – the way people often talk to foreigners as if they are deaf. Needless to say, he had not made a very good impression on me and I didn't think I had made much of an impression on him either. I hadn't had much to do with him after that, so I couldn't think what he might want to talk to me about. Unless it was the fact that I thought one of his friends liked my friend – this had been a big topic of conversation between Sandie and me for a few weeks.

When I finished my cleaning duty I ran to Sandie's room quickly to tell her about the weird conversation I'd had with Michael, the German. Telling her that I thought it was about a matchmaking opportunity for her she looked at me and laughed.

'Claudette, are you sure?' she asked.

I was adamant I was right, but Sandie sat quietly and smiled.

The Walk and the Talk

When evening came and we went down to the dining hall for dinner, I looked for Michael but he wasn't there. I sat at the table waiting until six o'clock, when he finally came out of his side of the halls of residence. Together we went outside and walked through the campus. There was a fish pond on the pathway leading out of the grounds and as we neared it he tried to speak.

'I . . . I . . .' he stammered.

I could see that he was nervous so I tried to reassure him, 'It's OK, Michael.'

Being sure that he was going to ask about the chances for his friend, I couldn't understand why he'd be so nervous about it.

'I . . . I . . . I, erm . . .'

He was blushing and we stopped walking. I placed my hand on his shoulder to reassure him as he looked lost for words.

'It's alright Michael; I'm your sister in the Lord. You can talk to me,' I said, trying to be mature, motherly and very, very Christian.

Finally he cleared his throat and spoke, his face turning bright red in the process.

'I . . . I . . . like you very much and want to marry you. I have prayed and fasted for ten days, and God told me that we are to marry and you will be my wife.'

I nearly fell into the pond, the shock was so great. I was speechless. I could not believe that it was happening again. First, God told Sista to be my friend and now he was telling someone to marry me. The whole situation was crazy, unbelievable, impossible, madness.

We started to walk again and as we walked, he talked. He talked solidly for nearly thirty minutes all about how God had told him that he was to marry a black woman, but not just any black woman – me. He said he had known from the age of 14 that he was to marry outside of his race and he even started talking about having children, using affirmative language such as 'when we are married'. When? I thought. I hadn't even said yes, and this man, no – this boy – had already set a date, had children, grandchildren and was sitting in his rocking chair handing out Werther's Originals. I couldn't speak due to the shock and didn't say a word until we got back to campus.

To me it was ridiculous, and as we stood at the door of the halls of residence I knew that I would never marry him. I was sure this was just God's way of trying to boost my self-esteem. My Father had heard me moan the night before and had sent Michael to ask me to marry him; at least I was attractive to somebody. My honest-to-goodness thought was, 'How sweet of the Lord to try to cheer me up.' It had worked, as I was smiling, and for a few minutes I lost track of what Michael was saying as I held my own private conversation with God in my head, thanking him for the confidence boost but saying a definite 'No, thank you' to the proposal.

Finally, Michael asked me something and I was jolted back to listening to him. I sighed, knowing that I had to let him down gently. However, tact was not my forte then – or now. I decided to act in the best 'womanistic' way I could, which was about as 'gentle' as any black woman who meant business could be.

'*God* may have told *you* about marriage, but he hasn't said anything to *me*.' Michael looked slightly bewildered as I continued, 'And just because God said that it was to be a black woman, he didn't mean that it had to be the *first* black woman you met after leaving Germany!'

Bar moving my head from side to side, it was a performance similar to the mother in the US sitcom *Everybody Hates Chris*. I was formidable and frightening, and when I think of it now I shudder at my lack of grace considering the courage it took him to approach me. Nevertheless, at the time I believed I had to be firm with him because I would never even entertain the idea of a relationship with him. No way! Not in a million, billion, trillion, zillion, whatever 'illion' years. I shook my head and point-blank refused to consider Michael as a prospective husband.

It was fear that made me act that way, and deep down I was terrified of this apparently sincere young man. I wasn't going to marry him and I told him so. I didn't know him and I certainly didn't trust him. He was a skinny German student with very poor taste in clothes and a severe haircut. I didn't say all that to him, of course, but I definitely thought it. I left it at that, but he still asked me to think about his proposal and not to discuss it with anyone.

Well, forgive me, but I did discuss it with someone. Like any young woman who gets a sudden marriage proposal I ran straight to my best friend to tell her everything. I squealed at the preposterousness of the situation and lay on Sandie's bed laughing hysterically. Although she was surprised, Sandie gave a thoughtful smile as if she didn't think it was as crazy as I did. I started to think that she knew something I didn't, and sat up. She asked me if I was going to accept. I couldn't believe that she would even think I'd consider it. Of course I wasn't going to accept. I didn't know him at all and you can't just ask someone to marry you – besides, he didn't ask, he just told me we'd get married. I may not have had much in the way of romantic notions of love and marriage but I knew that I wanted a bit more of a courtship than, 'I like you and vee vill get married' (German accent).

After I had chewed it over sufficiently with Sandie I went back to my room, but I couldn't rest so I ran over to the same phone box I had used the night before and called Sista. I practically screamed down the phone as I told her about it and said that I thought that it was just God being nice to me after my bellyaching the day before. She laughed, but before I could continue with my theory she quickly said, 'Just don't say no.'

I couldn't believe it. I thought she would at least see it my way. I told her that it was impossible and asked her why I shouldn't say no. I wasn't even attracted to him and I was also too scared to contemplate a relationship – after all, he didn't want a girlfriend, he wanted a *wife*. Michael had even revealed to me that he had never had a girlfriend and hadn't even kissed a girl. When he talked to me he had clearly prepared a speech about himself and what he told me confirmed that there was no way I should consider a relationship with him.

Michael was a middle-class pastor's kid, whereas I was the daughter of a former cleaner and a profligate, alcoholic barber. He'd had a strict upbringing with no television until the age of 14. My upbringing was strict, but I had also experienced things that someone like him could never understand. He seemed very spiritual and talked of fasting and praying all the time. Although I prayed, I was certainly not one of those 'lock myself in the closet and pray for ten hours a day' types of Christian. He had a passion for mission and didn't seem to care about material things, whereas I was very fashion conscious, having nearly four wardrobes full of clothes and a growing collection of shoes. As a student I trawled through charity shops to find glamorous bargains. Our dissimilarities were abundant. He was all innocence and holiness, and in comparison I was worldly and cynical. I knew that he would not be able to handle me and all my baggage. Besides, he didn't just want to get to know me, he wanted to marry me, and I could never imagine telling someone so virtuous about my past. We were not just opposites in colour, nationality and culture, but in social standing and personal history. We had little in common, with the only middle ground being that we shared the same faith. It seemed ridiculous that he wanted to marry me because he believed that God had told him to.

I explained all this to Sista and she pointed out that something like it had happened before, referring to the book of Hosea in the Bible. But I rejected that comparison, as God told Hosea to marry a prostitute. She used a biblical precedent to try to help me see it was not as unusual or as crazy as I thought but, as ever, I focused on the negative and was offended at being compared with that type of woman. I dismissed it. As far as I was concerned either God had to be joking or Michael had made a mistake, and I was sure that Michael had got it wrong. After a long conversation with Sista we ended the call but her last words to me were, 'Just don't say no, not yet.' I told her I would think about it, but deep down inside I rejected the foreign young man who believed God had told him to marry me.

I was so perturbed by what he had said that I went to Johnnie and Enid's house and told them about it. Johnnie was not surprised. He said that he could tell Michael had been 'sweet' on me and he had seen it coming; he thought that he was a nice lad and was just the type of person I needed in my life. I was amazed. When I got back to campus I then told Calvin and he too seemed to think that Michael would be good for me. It felt like a conspiracy. I didn't agree. Although by that time some of them did know about parts of my past, no one knew all of it, and I believed that if they did they would see just how unequal a match it would be.

By late evening all of my friends knew about it and when we met up in the common room after ten, as was our habit, Michael was there too. The innuendos and furtive looks were obvious, and I'm surprised he didn't find out then that I had told them. (He now knows, when it comes to matters of the heart, never to ask a girl not to tell anyone – she has to tell her friends, it's the female code.)

By this time I had good friends and even though I still struggled when they occasionally disappointed me, as friends do, they never rejected me and they accepted me for who I was. Most importantly, they forgave me when I let them down, and through them God not only showed me fatherly love but the love of friends as well. I thought that this was all the love I needed, however, and I convinced myself that I was happy with that. I was certainly not ready to accept the kind of love Michael had in mind. That was a love too far.

The next day I felt happy; it gave me a real buzz to know someone liked me. Even though I had convinced myself that I would never marry him, I couldn't help but watch him. And while I did I tried to find reasons to dislike him. First, I critiqued his image. He seemed to have poor dress sense and wore brown shoes with white socks, burgundy trousers and loud Hawaiian shirts – a definite candidate for *What Not to Wear*. Then I focused on his grasp of the English language, which was limited. The fact that he was German and white gave me more reasons to see the unlikelihood of the match. Yet Sista's words kept haunting me. I knew what she meant. She wanted me to give him a fighting chance. I called her again to talk it through and hoped to convince her that it would never work, but instead of agreeing she quietly encouraged me just to get to know him.

I have to say that there was a reason why other men at the college never approached me, and it was not because I was unattractive, which was what I believed. It was because I would give them a dose of my 'womanism' if they tried. I was very abrupt whenever it came to matters of the heart, and had a tough reputation in college as someone who took no prisoners as far as men were concerned. I purposely intimidated the young men; I have to admit that I enjoyed it. I suppose I was exacting some sort of revenge for the pain of the past, yet I couldn't see the silliness of my behaviour. However, I couldn't help who I was, even though it made me unapproachable. It was only when I started to yearn for a boyfriend after Calvin's letter from

God that I knew I was partly to blame for the lack of attention. But by then it was too late: my reputation as a man-hater was set. So Michael's proposal was braver than you can imagine.

Pros and Cons

I had many discussions with Calvin and Sandie, and then Johnnie and Enid, as well as Sista, separately, but they all told me that I should try to get to know Michael a bit better. It felt very much like all my friends had schemed against me, rooting for Michael. I disagreed and continued to watch him with suspicion. Eventually I made up my mind that I was going to say no to him, but every time I tried I found I lacked the courage. So I just didn't say anything and for the next week until half-term, whenever we bumped into each other we barely talked. He didn't mention his proposal again, but every day in morning chapel he'd politely nod and smile at me.

It was then I began to notice that he had a certain *something* about him – a gentility and charm that I did quite like. As I watched him I could see such kindness in his smile, and when we did talk we always seemed to end up laughing. He made me laugh and that couldn't be bad, but whenever my thoughts strayed that way I would try to snap them back, returning to the list of faults that I could see. Some days I could see only negative things, the next I could see the positive. I had a pros and cons list, but in the end the biggest con was me.

I believed that if he got to know the real me he would reject me just as my father had done, and I couldn't let that happen. So I prayed and asked the Lord what to do. Yes, I wanted a friend, a special friend, and I thought I had found that in Sista, but there was no way that Michael could be 'The One'. Every girl at some point thinks of the one person they could love for the rest of their lives, but whoever I had envisaged it certainly wasn't him. Of course, I had noticed him as he was very handsome, but rather boyish looking. He was slim, athletic, with tanned olive skin and the most striking blue eyes I had ever seen. And, of course, he had *that* smile, one that everybody warmed to, and together with his brilliant blue eyes he charmed everyone that met him. In the months that followed our unfortunate introduction in the kitchen I had even teased him about his lovely eyes, even though he was not my type. If I had a type that I was looking for I would probably have set the bar at Denzel Washington; whenever I did imagine the man of my dreams he was mature, dark (and by that I mean black) and handsome. Michael was indeed handsome, but he did not fit the rest of my criteria.

The main problem for me was that we were from such different backgrounds. I was sure it could never work and my prayers became like arguments for him but against myself, and I didn't know what to do. After lots of conferences with my friends a decision had to be made. Calvin insisted that I couldn't go on half-term break and leave Michael unsure as to where he stood. Every time he walked past me he looked like a little boy who wanted to know whether he was going to get the present he'd asked for. My friends all wanted me to say yes. Johnnie and Enid were sure that Michael was the right kind of man for me. Calvin and Sandie were convinced that he was the sweetest guy and that I should get to know him, but I knew that they didn't have any idea of what Michael would be getting into if I said yes.

Ten days had passed by since his proposal and half-term had arrived, so I had to give Michael an answer before we departed. Sandie and I were going to Sista's house for the week, and with much fear I agreed to try to get to know him a little better. I was not going to marry him, but I wanted to make friends with him – and that was all. With this resolve I finally had an answer. It was an hour before we were due to leave and I knew I had to tell him something, but I was so nervous that I decided to write a note and give it to him instead. The problem was that I didn't know what to write, so my first 'love note' to Michael was composed by . . . Calvin. Yes, a man dictated to me what to write (Michael didn't know this until months later, and it is now a story that he and Calvin tell with great amusement).

As the college emptied for the May break I handed him the note and we went our separate ways. I didn't know what he would think of my note, which thanked him for his proposal but said that although I would not commit to marrying him I would like us to be friends and get to know each other. I gave him my phone number at Sista's house and thought that I (or should I say Calvin) had made it clear that it was very early days and I wanted to take it slowly. I awaited his call nervously.

The following day, in the afternoon, the phone rang. Sista answered it and passed it to me, mouthing silently, 'It's him.' I stood in the hallway with the door open so she and Sandie could listen and give me support. I said hello and asked Michael if he had read my note and he said that he had. I was relieved, as it meant that he understood we were not to mention marriage. I waited for him to say something, but neither of us spoke and the silence was dreadful. Minutes seemed to pass by and I didn't know what to make of it when, suddenly, he blurted out the words – I love you.

It was then I thought that either this guy can't read English or he's as thick as two short planks, because for him to use the word 'love' was too much – it was terrifying. I knew he was absolutely *not* the one for me. I thought he was stark raving mad and didn't know what he was doing.

But I couldn't have been further from the truth. I was unaware of the process that Michael had gone through before he approached me. In reality he was so sure that we were to marry, that he was ready to run full steam ahead regardless of what I said or wrote. Plus, I underestimated the determination of the 21-year-old German called Michael Schlitter . . .

13
It Started With a Kiss

A kiss is a lovely trick designed by nature to stop speech when words become superfluous.

Ingrid Bergman

From our very first meeting in the kitchen Michael had noticed me. He initially thought that I came across as quite forthright and confident, but soon noticed that there was something about me that was lost and sad. During his first six months as a student he made a point of looking out for me, and he couldn't quite figure out what it was but felt drawn to me. He was not the type of man to act rashly and took full advantage of the relationship rule that was in force. New students were not allowed to start a relationship in their first six months. It sounds a bit draconian now, but we accepted it. So when he first came to Mattersey in September 1993, Michael was not permitted to ask me out, although I was in my second year.

I didn't know that I was being observed and was just being myself. Suffering from PMS, mood swings, anaemia, poor health and family problems at home I was not always a lovely sight. At the times when Sandie, Calvin and I would sit and chat, unbeknown to me Michael was watching me. Intrigued by the apparent contradiction of my confident outward persona and the vulnerable moments I shared with my friends, he found himself caring about the woman he had inadvertently called 'Closet'.

During the Easter break Sandie had taken me home with her to Ireland but on the way there we were involved in a car accident and I suffered a whiplash injury. I rang my mother from the ferry port to tell her, but before I could she told me that my sister and her husband were getting a divorce. It was upsetting news as they had two small children and because of that I decided not to tell her about the accident, as she had enough to worry about. We both always tried to shield each other from bad news and I went to Ireland extremely upset both about the accident and that my sister's marriage had fallen apart. It seemed to me that good men were still in short supply and I was very upset for my sister. It strengthened my 'womanist' resolve and I vowed never to get married.

The Master's Plan

It was April 1994, and the six-month relationship rule was at an end for Michael. By then he was sure that the young woman that he'd been watching was 'The One'. After taking ten days out to pray and fast he was convinced, and he chose his moment carefully, waiting for the opportune time to approach. Unfortunately, he chose the week after I had travelled back from Ireland. We were both part of a group of students representing the college at the Assemblies of God annual conference. One day I was sitting in the meeting room in-between services and he sat next to me. I didn't notice him, as I was lost in my own thoughts of my sister and was in a lot of pain due to the whiplash I had suffered. This felt like his moment and, plucking up the courage, he was about to speak to me when he felt God tell him not to, not just yet. As eager as Michael was to ask me to marry him, he was obedient to the prompting that God had given him that his timing was off – way off. He was right, as due to the state of mind I was in I would have rejected him immediately. Instead he decided to wait, watch and pray.

When we went back to the college for the next term he tried to befriend me, and I, unaware of his intentions, would tease him about his beautiful blue eyes. Somehow he always seemed to be around where I was, and Johnnie had noticed. Whenever we met I would mention his eyes and I thought it was harmless fun. I never imagined him to be interested in me, yet all the while he continued to pray and ask God for the right time to approach me.

Then came the day I moaned to Sista about my desire to have someone like me, and that was also the day that Michael heard that it was the right time. God's timing is perfect, and he told Michael to ask me the next day. With little eloquence, he obeyed God and the proposal by the pond took place. So by the time I had given him my note he was positive my answer was going to be yes. He read it and was not disappointed, as even though I hadn't said yes he believed it would only be a matter of time. He was confident that our relationship was to be, because he was confident in the Master's plan.

During our telephone conversation, however, when he said those three frightening words, 'I love you', I really didn't know what to say. I just wanted to get off the phone. When he said goodbye he told me that I was beautiful and once again said that he loved me. At that I panicked and it felt as though he was a runaway train on a collision course with me. The resultant emotional chaos caused by Michael's declaration of love involved me talking to Sandie non-stop about how crazy he was. I remember being so scared that night that I cried myself to sleep and asked God for help, as there was a crazy German on some kind of mission to marry me. I questioned God about how he could tell Michael but not say a word about it to me. Didn't I have a say on the matter? What Michael wanted was far too over-whelming for me to accept and I decided that when I saw him again I would tell him that I didn't want to see him – either as a friend or a potential life partner.

A week later, back on campus, I waited nervously in the dining room, hoping to see him. I braced myself for the task ahead, determined this time to be kind but firm and to let him down gently. When he arrived, though, his smile and manner were so genuine that my resolve melted. I for-got my prepared speech and sat down to talk to him. I don't know how it happened, but somehow Michael and I began our cautious courtship.

Ours was a very quiet, understated relationship, and no one who saw us would have thought that a budding romance was taking place. We met in the evenings to go for walks off-campus, and that was *all* we did. We walked and tried to talk, but had a lot of difficulty understanding each other. He seemed very abrupt and said that I was always apologizing for everything – and that was very English. I thought him ill-mannered, curt and confident, bordering on arrogant. Even though within the Caribbean Islands there are cultural differences, and I was the product of a mixed relationship with my father being from Jamaica and my mother from Barbados, these were minuscule differences in comparison to the racial barrier Michael and I faced. We were very much children of our respective ethnicities, and although there would still have been issues if I had met a white Englishman, with the added language barrier and cultural differences the issues seemed almost insurmountable. Plus, no matter what I said, I couldn't get across to him that I was not ready to accept that he was The One for me just because God had told *him* so.

The more we talked the more evident it became that we were from opposing spheres in every respect, even down to our perspectives on life. Michael had a very positive disposition and I still had a negative core running through me. Remnants from the years of bullying and assault made me doubt his sincerity. He was ultra-confident in his faith and in himself, and he could not understand why I wasn't the same. It seemed to me that he had led a charmed life whilst I'd had nothing but heartache and rejection. I didn't think he really knew that to love me was to take all of me, warts and all, and not just the born-again me. Yet I also didn't want to offer him all of me, so I told him nothing about my past, believing he would never understand or would be disgusted by what he heard.

Michael now admits that he really didn't know what he was getting into, or who this woman was that he wanted to marry. All he knew was that God had spoken to him and that he was to love me, and he tried, but I made it very difficult. At times I was also abrupt, and positive in only one thing – that it would never work. We had little in common, and it showed.

First Date

We continued in our old-fashioned courtship of walking out together for a couple of weeks until one day Calvin suggested we have a real first date. So, one weekend when his fiancée Sarah was visiting, the four of us went to York for the day. The relationship was going nowhere fast, and Calvin played matchmaker knowing that if we didn't get our act together soon it was likely that love between us was never going to happen. Certainly, I was ready to give up. In my mind, the date would either make or break us.

We got on well enough – Michael was kind, funny and good-looking, and we could talk about general topics, but it was obvious to both of us that we had nothing in common apart from our faith and I didn't think that would be enough. As far as attraction went I was not feeling it and I was sure his was waning for me. I couldn't even imagine kissing him, let alone holding hands. Deep down inside, however, I was a secret romantic at heart. I loved old-fashioned films and musicals, and I longed for what I had seen in the movies. The only experiences I'd had with boys so far had been unpleasant and I wanted that classic, arched back, one-foot-up-in-the-air kind of kiss and romance. I wanted the memories of the past obliterated in a kiss, and felt that if he were indeed The One then his kiss would do it. Michael had already told me he had never kissed a girl, and I, unfortunately, had more experience than he did, but I thought that maybe if we did kiss there was a chance that there might be the chemistry we needed. So I made up my mind to bring up the subject on our first date, believing if it could somehow magically erase the past then we were meant to be. It was a tall order for a simple kiss; Sleeping Beauty, but with no guarantee of awakened love afterwards.

When Michael got into the car for the journey to York and I saw how he was dressed, I cringed. He was wearing a very loud Hawaiian shirt tucked into his jeans, hitched up high by a contrasting striped blue and white belt. The ensemble was complete with white socks and scruffy trainers. I, on the other hand, had taken great care and attention in my outfit. Everything matched and my hair was done 'just so', but he looked as if he couldn't be bothered to make an effort for our first official date. It felt like an ominous sign of things to come. On the way there the four of us chatted comfortably, but when we arrived I felt my nerves prickle when Calvin and Sarah decided to go their separate way and Michael and I were alone. We walked around the city and he cautiously held my hand. His hand was sweaty and I could tell that he was nervous too. For lunch we ate at a pizza restaurant and things began to improve as we slowly started to interpret each other's verbal nuances and colloquialisms.

After lunch we sat on the old city wall and watched people as they went by. Once again, the conversation dried up. The setting was right and romantically sunlit; York was full of history, the location memorable, with pretty surroundings. It was a perfect place for a first kiss and there seemed no better time to broach the subject. I took a deep breath, plucked up the courage, and told him that he could kiss me if he wanted to. Michael looked surprised; he paused to think for what seemed an age and then finally said OK. I got ready for what I hoped would be the kiss of my dreams, something that could change our relationship from one of wary companions to loving duo. I closed my eyes in anticipation, but moments passed and nothing happened. The tension was tangible, so I leaned forward, and he didn't seem to know what to do – so technically, I think I kissed him. His lips met mine and within seconds it was over.

It was a disaster.

It was disastrous because there were no hearts and flowers, chemistry or awakened love. It was juvenile and really disappointing. It was truly one of the worst kisses. He had told me that he had never kissed a girl before, and boy was he was telling the truth. I hadn't kissed anyone in eight years but I could not believe a kiss could be so bad. I asked him what he thought about it, as his face was bright red and he looked visibly shocked, and then he said it.

'I feel like Joseph after Potiphar's wife tried to tempt him.'

Talk about adding insult to injury. In all seriousness, he was practically accusing me of trying to seduce him. My Christian sensibilities were offended and I was mortified. It could not have gone worse and we got up from our seats and resumed our walk in silence. We hardly spoke until we met up with Calvin and Sarah at the end of the day. After a subdued journey home we went to our respective rooms, not really speaking. It had been a disastrous first date.

It's In His Kiss

The next day was Sunday and I didn't want to see him, so I deliberately stayed in my room until Michael had left for his church. I went to my assigned placement and was away the whole day, returning after nine at night. All day I knew I had to end it; it would never work. When I got back to campus I went straight to my room to try to think things through. He had not returned yet and I was quite relieved, hoping that I would not have to see him until the next day. I dreaded telling him that I could not see him any more. In fact, the whole courtship was becoming very arduous and the more I thought about him, the more I believed I was right. It had to be done, for there was no spark between us. I couldn't love him, or even find common ground, and when we kissed there was no chemistry. God wanted me to be open to love and I had succeeded as far as my friendships were concerned, but it was impossible with Michael.

I was lost in my thoughts when I heard a knock at the door. It was one of the other girls in my halls and she said that Michael was outside waiting for me. I didn't really want to see him and as I descended the stairs my heart felt heavy in the knowledge that our somewhat awkward romance was ending, after just two weeks.

It was late at night and the main campus lights were out, so the only light available was the full moon. It was beaming down on him as he stood underneath an old oak tree. Initially, I thought my eyes were playing tricks on me in the moonlight. He was stunningly handsome, dressed in a blue jacket that complemented his eyes, a crisp white shirt and smart tie complete with gold tie-pin. His pressed black trousers and polished black shoes were a marked difference to the clothes that I had seen previously. I couldn't believe it was the same man as the day before, as he was immaculately dressed. I didn't know it then but he was dressed smartly because he had been preaching. Even with his Bible in one hand, looking the part of the well-groomed young preacher, however, I was still prepared to finish the relationship. Looks weren't everything, and there was no passion or chemistry between us. In regret, I sighed and walked towards him.

When I was about a metre away from him I got ready to tell him it was over. But before I could say anything he put out his hand, placed it on the small of my back and pulled me close to him. He was holding me gently, I looked up in surprise, and then he bent his head downwards and kissed me. Every romance novel I'd read, and every romantic scene I'd ever watched paled into insignificance compared to that kiss. Full of passion and with a tenderness that told me I was his; his kiss was everything I had wished for and more. It was soft, tender and gave instead of taking. As he held me in his arms I knew that Michael would not hurt me. I had never been kissed with love before, and that was the power of his kiss, his love. Then he let me go. I felt lightheaded and dazed. I stared at the 'new' Michael who had just blown me away with his kiss.

'Sorry I grabbed you like that, but I didn't want to give you a chance to speak,' he said, as if he knew that I was about to break off the relationship.

I was breathless and asked him, 'Where did you learn to kiss like that? Have you been practising in the mirror?'

He shook his head, laughed, and said that he had thought about how to kiss and then just 'got' it. I later found out that this is one of Michael's character traits. He might not get some things at first, but if you give him time to assimilate something new he will become very good at it.

He smiled, knowing that he had been successful in his kiss, quickly said goodnight and, just like in the old movies, he turned and walked away. He left me standing there as I watched him glide suavely back to his room. He had truly swept me off my feet and, unbelievably, my foot did go up when he kissed me. When I went back to my room I fell backwards onto the bed and silently screamed, '*Wow!*'

It sounds unbelievable and clichéd, but it was then that I knew – I loved him.

I didn't know how I could love him so quickly, but I did, and it terrified me. I am an incurable romantic now, but back then I was afraid of love, and for me to even *think* that

I loved him at such an early stage was alarming. I didn't understand him, and he certainly didn't get me, but somehow God had put him in my life.

A new love had begun, and it all started with a kiss.

14
The Vacillating Heart

I am black, but comely . . .

Song of Solomon 1:5 (KJV)

Autumn had arrived and I had to learn to let the leaves fall. The coat of fear of rejection had to come off, otherwise I would never be able to let Michael love me and I would never truly love him. But I resolved not to tell Michael that I thought I was falling for him. I didn't want him to be in a position of power over me, and if I told him he would know he had the ability to break my heart. So I fought the love I felt every step of the way. Sometimes I tried to be mean to him just to prove that he would reject me, and there were days when I made myself so obnoxious and unloveable that I don't know how he persevered. (He later told me that with his limited grasp of English he really didn't understand half of the sarcastic jibes that I directed at him. Now he gives as good as he gets.)

Six weeks had gone by since his proposal and, although it was the early stages of our relationship, we had to separate. The summer holidays had arrived and Michael was to return to Germany for three months. A long separation in the early stages of getting to know someone is not good, and it proved hard. I worked at the college again for a few weeks and then spent time at home in Birmingham. All the while we corresponded by letter as I didn't have a computer with easy access to email, as so many of us do today. I tried to hide the relationship from my family in case it failed, and after two months of letter writing I started to have serious doubts. There were frequent misunderstandings, along with quite a few deliberate insults from me, and by the end of the three months apart we had reached the point where once again I thought that the relationship could not work. In one letter I had been so acerbic, in fact, that in the last few weeks of the summer break all I received from Michael was one postcard, with no sentiment attached. Then all correspondence stopped.

I thought I would be happy that the rejection I had expected from him had finally come, proving my belief that men let you down, but I wasn't. It dawned on me that I did want to have a relationship with him, although I was still unsure whether he was the one for me. I didn't think I was worthy of him and thought he would be repulsed if he knew about my past. The racial and cultural differences were the least of my worries; I had such low self-esteem that I believed I wasn't good enough for someone like him. I had to make a definite decision as to whether to pursue the relationship. Surely this love couldn't be from God, could it? Michael said that God had spoken to him about me and that he had fasted and prayed about it, so I decided to do the same. If it worked for him, why not me?

It was a big decision, as I had not fasted from food since my recovery from bulimia. I had always abstained from other things, such as television or a luxury, but not food. The temptation to diet and become obsessive about food was always too great, but this issue weighed so heavily on my heart that I made up my mind to do it.

I spent one day fasting and asked God whether Michael was really the man for me. His ultimate aim was marriage, and marriage could not be based on a powerful kiss or a fuzzy feeling in the pit of my stomach. I needed to know if it was right. Needless to say, I waited all day for some kind of revelation to come but none did. I think I expected a divine appearance with angels and harps attached, which would have probably terrified me. I finished the day none the wiser about what to do.

The Sunday before I was to return to college and see Michael again I went to my home church in Hockley and sat close to the back, feeling quite depressed. Our romance was summed up in his final postcard: brief and with limited capacity. I sat in church and declared to God that I could not accept Michael. His love felt like it was being imposed on me. How could it be from God?

That's Me!

That Sunday we had visiting speakers from overseas, Art and Greta Sheppard, who together shared from the Bible, with Greta speaking first. I really didn't take in what she was saying, or even bother to open my Bible, as she asked the congregation to turn to Song of Solomon. I was still questioning God and just kept my head down, wondering if there was going to be a future for Michael and me. The very next thing that she said made me sit bolt upright, however, and open my Bible quicker than I could say, 'That's me!'

And in the Song of Solomon it's the story of a king fallen in love with a . . . now she says her skin was dark, and there's much speculation as to her race, but it sounds almost like she would be black and he would be white . . . And because of the difference between them . . . she walks away from him. And he calls to her constantly and she won't answer him, but he longs for her to come right into his arms. And it is these differences that make her vacillate, this feeling of unworthiness.

'He's the king, I'm just me. He's up there and I'm down there.' And you know that mentality is in us. We feel so unworthy to come to him . . .

Greta Sheppard

Well, pardon my Brummie, but I bloomin' well nearly fell off my seat as she began to read from the passage of Scripture and elaborate on it. I frantically turned the pages of my Bible with my heart pounding, scrambling to get my notepad and pen to write it down and dropping everything in the process. Greta continued:

And so in this Song of Solomon . . . It's the beloved, the King saying to the girl . . . he loves her . . . he wants her. And she's pulling back and pulling back, and he's waiting for her to avail herself to him . . . he sees her as a garden, like she's put a padlock on the garden gate of her heart and she won't let him come in . . . God sees potential in us and we pull back, saying, 'Oh, not me lord, I can't speak, I can't witness, I can't do that Lord, I'm just . . .' [But] he sees her prophetically, what she could be. And God sees all the potential that's in your life today, and he's saying, 'Where have you been? Please unlock your garden.'

Then she . . . realizes what she has done . . . she has locked her garden up and sealed her fountain and given him no access . . . and then she says, 'Awake, north wind, and come, south wind! Blow on my garden, that its fragrance may spread everywhere' (Song 4:16).

Do you know that the north wind speaks of change? But it also speaks of the word of conviction – biting north winds – they bite, they sting, they wake you up . . . because conviction always brings change. North winds always speak of a change in the weather. God wants to change your weather today and he wants to blow over your life.

Whereas the north wind is cold and convicting . . . the south wind is warm and comforting . . . often bringing soothing rain. Flowers close up when the air is cold; no fragrance is available. Warm air and the gentle touching of soft rain opens them up so their fragrance can be enjoyed by others. It makes sense, therefore, that we can find the fragrance of forgiveness more easily in warm breezes rather than in chilling, biting winds of angry feelings.

Greta Sheppard

You may wonder how I remember this so clearly: I bought the cassette recording of the talk and have it with me to this day.* Although she was talking about intimacy in worship, I also knew that God was showing me my situation with

---

* The extracts are taken from a transcript of a message from Greta Sheppard, recorded at Hockley Pentecostal Church on Sunday 11 September 1994, from a cassette entitled *Intimacy and Worship* (Still Waters Tapes, REF-HPC.34588M).

Michael as well. I was scared of allowing Michael to love me, but the comparisons in the passage she read were too powerful to ignore. I was just like the woman in Song of Solomon, too afraid to let love in, afraid of the north wind of change and the south wind's fragrances of forgiveness. This was the confirmation I had asked God for, but it wasn't the answer I truly wanted. I had a million arguments as to why the relationship wouldn't work, but God wanted me to be open to love and Michael was part of that. Yet, I had a vacillating heart, one that had drawn to him and pulled away. I thought that I had blown it, and just like the woman in Song of Solomon who had locked the door to her heart and garden, I thought I had locked mine.

She Loves Me, She Loves Me Not

Calvin had arranged to pick up Michael and another student, Jimmy, from the airport at the end of the summer break, although after I told him about the disastrous summer correspondence he hatched a plan that I would go with him to Heathrow Airport to meet Michael. I hoped that I could repair the damage that I'd done, but I had pulled back and forth with Michael so much that I wasn't sure he would even want to speak to me. When he finally came off the plane and met us I was heartbroken, as he hugged Calvin and Jimmy but then put out his hand to shake mine. He didn't even attempt to kiss me on the cheek or show any kind of affection, and I thought that I had lost him forever. I had vacillated too much and he no longer wanted me.

My initial reaction was that I wanted to get as far away from him as possible but, remembering the message I'd heard, I knew I couldn't. I couldn't let fear rule my life any more. I had to let him know that I wanted to be with him. Calvin was witness to the frosty atmosphere between us and, ever the matchmaker, he took us to lunch. Michael talked to Calvin and Jimmy about his holiday but said little to me. Then, towards the end of the meal Calvin suddenly announced that he and Jimmy had somewhere to go and they left, but before they did Calvin gave me a conspiratorial brotherly look, ordering me to talk to Michael and put things right. We sat in awkward silence, each waiting for the other to say something. Finally, I knew I had to break the ice.

'I'm sorry Michael,' I said, and was about to try to explain my caustic letters, but when I looked into his eyes I knew what I had to say. I couldn't pretend any more.

'I think I could love you, Michael, but I'm scared. I was horrible to you in my letters because I'm scared of all this, and of you.'

I then told him about the message that I had heard on Sunday morning and tried to make him see that I wasn't an awful person – I had just experienced awful things and was fearful. However, he didn't speak or show any facial reaction to what I was saying. I continued to talk and fumbled my way through my words. I struggled when I looked at his face, as it showed no sign of softening, and I thought that I had blown it. I felt sure he was going to end the relationship before it had even really begun. Even if God had told him to marry me, he must have thought that I was too unstable and emotional a person to be with. I stopped talking and I held my head down in dread, awaiting his negative response.

'I haven't given up on you,' he said, 'I just wasn't sure where I stood, and needed time to think.'

He put out his hand and grabbed mine but said no more on the subject as we paid the bill and left the restaurant. As we walked he held my hand, but didn't talk, and I wasn't sure what to make of it until he stopped in his tracks and turned to me.

'Let's start all over again from here,' he said, 'as if the last three months hadn't happened.' He had been quiet because he had been deep in thought.

I was not going to play the game of 'she loves me, she loves me not' any more. As we walked, I squeezed his hand as a sign of trust. I had to trust God that the love Michael was offering was for real and, although I was very nervous, I agreed to start afresh. I didn't know the first thing about having a real relationship but I was willing to try.

After that Michael and I, along with his friend Jimmy, spent three days with Calvin and his mother at her home, where I started to get to know the strange young German. What I mistook for arrogance when he declared to a relative stranger that she was to be his wife, was really an unwavering faith. The differences that previously seemed so insurmountable disappeared as I saw he had a heart that was open and honest. His beliefs were sure but his manner was humble, and the warmth of his smile broke down any uncertainty I had. His cheerful disposition lifted any mood, and as I got to know him I saw we had more in common than I had thought. I stopped fighting the feeling of love that had frightened me so much after he kissed me, and Michael won me over with his personality and charm. Slowly but surely, I found myself falling for him. When we got back to college we resumed our walks, but this time we talked openly. We shared our thoughts, dreams and desires.

A Promise to Love

One evening Michael and I sat in the entrance of a tiny chapel in the village and talked for hours. We had been getting to know each other for many months and I felt it was time to tell him the reasons why I had been so scared. I finally told him about the 'game', the bullies, The Boy, and my father, and by the time I finished I was crying. Then I said something that I hadn't planned to say.

'I'll give you my heart, and love you with everything I've got, but I beg you not to break it.' With tears streaming down my face I sobbed, 'Please, just don't break my heart.'

He wiped the tears from my face and held me as he comforted me. We sat silently for a while until he spoke. By then I had gotten used to Michael's long pauses to think, nevertheless I was still anxious to hear what he thought about my confession. He sighed as though the weight of my history had disturbed him, but then he spoke.

'I don't understand everything you've gone through, but I would never do to you what they did to you. You act tough, but I know you're extremely fragile and I promise I won't break your heart. I love you and want to take care of you. I still want to marry you, and I want you to be my wife.'

This time when he mentioned marriage, instead of feeling frightened I felt cherished. I believed his promise and I trusted him. I didn't realize that by allowing him to love me I was finally letting go of the past. I was no longer afraid to love or be loved. My defensive layers fell like autumn leaves, and I could at long last enjoy the season as my protective armour vanished. It took many months for me to take off each coat that had been covering me, but in order for me to let Michael love me as God wanted him to, change had to happen – and it did. I felt the beauty of God's love through this man. Someone loved me. Michael loved me: all of me, the good and the bad.

At times, I still had struggles with trust and my insecurities. A lot happened to us and we made mistakes, yet God continued to bless our relationship no matter how hard it got. I still had occasional doubts, and sometimes they would surface so strongly that I would attempt to break it off. Each time it was disastrous, as I was miserable without him. He became my best friend and we talked about everything and anything. We laughed a lot. Michael has a way of laughing that is infectious. He can be full of tears, with not a sound coming out of him, but with a wheeze and a squeal he keels over at something silly. He loves slapstick humour, especially the likes of Laurel and Hardy, and Mr Bean, and he taught me how to laugh at myself, as he always seemed to be laughing at me. I would say to him, 'I wish I could find myself so amusing,' and he would just smile, saying that I didn't know how funny I was.

I once asked him what he liked best about me, expecting him to say my singing, as most people did, but he didn't like me for my voice. In fact he never mentioned it, and at first I didn't even think he liked music. When he answered my question he paused to look at me with those intensely blue eyes of his and said, 'I love your honesty.' I was surprised, as no one had ever said that to me before, and then he went on to explain what he meant. He said that I try to cover up my emotions but I wear them on my face and I say what I think, and he loved that about me. He said I always tried to tell the truth about my feelings and if I couldn't I'd rather say so than lie. I smiled for days at that. Someone loved a part of my personality, my character, and had told me so.

Instead of calling me sensitive, he said I was caring. He said I loved a lot and gave my love completely once given, and that was why when I was rejected it hurt so much, because I expected everyone to give of themselves as much as I did. Never before had anyone sat and analysed me and found such good things to say.

He made me feel special, and still does.

After a few months we introduced each other to our respective families, although the story of our love and our relationship's highs, lows, comedies and errors are for another book. However, needless to say the inevitable happened, and in May 1995, whilst in a park in Doncaster, Michael got down on one knee and formally proposed – and I accepted. The ring was not very expensive but it is still the prize in my jewellery collection; yet Michael called me his prize, his beauty of beauties. He loved my hair, my dark chocolate skin, he even loved the curvaceous figure that I despised. For years I had thought myself unattractive, but here was a man who loved the things that the bullies had ridiculed.

A month later I graduated with distinction in my Diploma in Theology. Doreen, my old Sunday school leader who, along with other members of my church, had supported me financially throughout my three years at Bible college, was there to see me accept my diploma. I will never forget her smiling face on graduation day. Sista and her daughter came too, as well as friends from church, and of course my family. The support was amazing. My mother was finally able to see her baby's life improve for the better. It was a great day for the both of us, as she cheered me on in her own quiet way whilst I collected my certificate.

Compared to when I left school with no qualifications and no future, my life had certainly changed. I had completed three years of study, was engaged to be married, and had the love of my friends, family and church. All the people who had encouraged me to pursue my dreams, and even some who hadn't, were there that day. For the first time ever I cried because I was happy, and refreshing tears of joy streamed down my face. I was happy, I was loved, and I owed it all to God.

15
Falling Leaves

For he will command his angels concerning you to guard you in all your ways.

Psalm 91:11

Michael still had a year of studying to complete, so after graduation I went back home in order to work and prepare for our wedding. It was a long but busy year of preparation, although the time went quickly. However, the night before the wedding I got cold feet. The thought of the lifetime commitment we were making was very daunting and the prospect of matrimony at the age of 24 made me announce to Michael that I couldn't marry him. To my surprise, he said simply, 'OK.' I was rather taken aback, and thought that he wanted to call it off as well. Then he smiled, took me in his arms and spoke to me in the assertive way that only Germans can.

'Look Schatzi [treasure], you can call off the wedding if you want to but *I am going to marry you.* And if that means I have to wait for you one . . .' (he bent forward and kissed my nose between each number) '. . . two . . . or even ten years, I will wait for you to be ready. So,' he was laughing, 'you might as well marry me tomorrow and get it over and done with.'

At this we both laughed and I knew resistance was futile. I was bound to this crazy man no matter what, and so the wedding went ahead as scheduled the next day. On Saturday 6 July 1996 at Hockley Pentecostal Church, the church I had attended since the age of 5, I married the most wonderful man in the world. Johnnie gave me away, and I didn't miss having a father that day. Johnnie played the role perfectly. As I walked down the aisle and all eyes turned to watch me I felt beautiful because of one person's gaze; I had found someone who saw me as beautiful. Michael was in love with me. He loved me completely, without wanting to change anything, not even my weight. I believed that wedded bliss was a certainty and that nothing else could ever go wrong again.

We honeymooned on the continent for three weeks, spending time in Paris, Strasbourg, Amsterdam, Frankfurt and any other city we felt the urge to see. Michael showed me the sights of Europe across borders and we ate al fresco, buying baguettes in France whilst still able to hear dogs bark in Germany. We took boat rides in Amsterdam, drove through the high peaks of the Black Forest, and even stood at the top of the Eiffel Tower in Paris. It was a far cry from my school memories and the council estate in Birmingham where I grew up. My new husband opened my eyes to a world I had never seen before.

We had thought of living in Germany after our honeymoon, but Michael felt that God wanted us to stay in England, so we rented a small apartment in the north of Birmingham and settled down to married life. I went back to work at a water utility company where I was taking part in a graduate recruitment scheme. The role was temporary, but as I had already been there a year the possibility of being made a permanent member of staff was almost a certainty. I worked hard and was assured I would be appointed permanently to the post. This would have given us financial security, as Michael had only just graduated and had no imminent job prospects.

Dreaming

We had been married just over a month when one morning I sat up and said to Michael, 'Where's Chloe . . . Chloe Rose, where's the baby?' He looked at me as if I were going crazy and reassured me that I had been dreaming. When I finally woke up I realized that I had dreamt I had been holding the most beautiful little baby girl. Someone had asked me her name, to which I responded 'Chloe Rose'. I recalled her image vividly. She had light coffee-coloured skin, almond-shaped deep brown eyes, and a mat of straight black hair on her head. I told Michael about the dream, and something inside me said that it was either about to come true or already was.

A few weeks later I began to feel quite ill each morning – yes, you guessed it, I was pregnant. Because we hadn't planned to start a family so soon, I was scared. I wasn't sure if I had enough love to be a good mother, and told Michael so. I doubted my capacity to love anyone else as it had been such a struggle to allow myself to love him. What I didn't realize, however, was that love has no limits, as the longer I carried her the more I loved her. I was positive it was to be a girl – no one, not even a scan, would have been able to convince me otherwise – although Michael tried to prepare me for the possibility that it could be a boy.

A few weeks later we had been out for the evening and returned late to see a police car outside and all the lights on in our small flat. We had been burgled and most of the electrical wedding presents were gone, although fortunately the thieves left behind some things we had stored in a cupboard. The burglary was distressing and the next morning I woke to discover I had been bleeding. I went to the doctor, who spoke pragmatically.

'Some women miscarry and there is nothing that can be done. All you can do is go to bed and wait to see if you continue bleeding or not.'

I knew I had enough love for my child then, as I knew I didn't want to lose her – I loved her already. I stayed in bed for a few days and thankfully didn't lose the baby, but I did lose my job. I had worked there for more than a year but as soon as they found out I was pregnant, they let me go. At that point the law hadn't yet changed to give a temporary member of staff the same rights as permanent employees. This was the beginning of a number of bad employment experiences, resulting in insecurity and financial hardship, as Michael was still unemployed. Eventually he managed to get temporary work sorting parcels, but the money was poor and so were we. I couldn't get another job, as no one would employ a pregnant woman.

After six months of living in our flat we became increasingly unhappy. Neither of us felt comfortable enough to call it home, and life seemed to present one trial after another. So when a friend of ours offered us his place to rent, partly furnished, we snapped it up immediately. I wanted to move there because it was closer to my mother's and the city centre hospital where I was due to have the baby. Although it was compact it was a marked improvement, and we moved in hoping to prepare for our new arrival. We joined a church based outside the city and Michael was appointed leader of the evangelism team.

This was still a honeymoon period for us, in spite of the few setbacks we had experienced. The love that we had for each other and the prospect of becoming parents eclipsed any problems we faced – but little did we know that the drama had only just begun.

Ecstasy and Agony

We had been married for nearly eleven months when the day came for me to say the inevitable words, 'The baby's coming.' Michael didn't panic, although he was a little flustered. He stayed with me throughout the labour, which lasted for three long, exhausting days. It was worth it, though, and when they handed my baby girl to me I gasped at the resemblance to the baby in my dream. I knew just what to call her, and a very happy Michael agreed that her name should be Chloe Rose. She came into our lives on Monday 5 May 1997, the most amazing gift from God and the sweetest of children. She is beautiful inside and out, supremely gifted and talented, yet humble with it. I had never felt such love as the day I first held her in my arms; Michael and I were ecstatic.

When we got home two days later, all was excitement and chaos as visitors to see our gorgeous girl came and went. It was a joyous time, but secretly I was not enjoying it. I didn't feel very well but decided not to tell anyone about it, as I thought that was how all mothers felt after having a baby – exhausted. As ever, not wanting to admit I was struggling, I felt ill for several days but said nothing, hoping to feel better soon. On the fifth day things decidedly took a turn for the worse.

I was giving Chloe her morning feed, but with a throbbing headache couldn't wait to put her down just to be able to close my eyes. The morning daylight almost blinded me and, although Michael tried to ease the pain with an ice pack, soon I was writhing in agony and vomiting. A very worried Michael took me to hospital. He tried to take me to the maternity ward, but they refused to have me. The normal procedure was that any mother with an emergency up to ten days after labour should be readmitted into the maternity ward. Instead, I was sent to casualty where the care I received was little or non-existent. No one monitored or investigated my condition, and Michael had to pursue and pressure them to get someone to check me. I lay on a trolley all morning, being sick, and at one point the pain was so severe I thought I was dying and felt that if I just let go it would happen.

Finally, in the afternoon, when my midwife arrived I was taken to the maternity ward. She was furious that procedure had not been followed, but I was still left alone in a room by myself. No doctors had seen me and my blood pressure had been taken only once. Michael had been with me most of the day, but by then had gone to get Chloe, who was with my mother. He returned with both of them just in time, as my condition was deteriorating. He placed Chloe down to the left-hand side of my bed in her car seat, and I tried to turn to look at her, but as I moved I felt my eyes lock. I was sure I said to him that I couldn't move my eyes, but am told that I didn't actually say anything. The following account is what I heard from Michael, as I have no memory of it. I started to convulse violently and my mother screamed for the nurse. Michael watched in shock while I had a fit. Within seconds emergency buttons were pressed and a barrage of nurses and doctors attended to me, pushing him aside. It was a terrifying sight and at one point he thought he had lost me forever.

Not even a year married, with a five-day-old daughter, Michael was facing the prospect of losing his wife, and all he could do was pray. The doctors told him that I'd experienced an eclamptic seizure. A clot had formed at the back of my head and they were trying to thin my blood to see if it would disperse. The next forty-eight hours would be critical. They didn't know what state I would be in if I made it through. It was more than likely that I had suffered brain and kidney damage, and the prognosis was not good. He was told to expect the worst. He says that those two days were like a lifetime for him, and time stood still while he waited.

I was oblivious to the agony he was going through and lay in intensive care fighting for my life. I have no memory of it, apart from when I occasionally regained consciousness. I had been given a muscle relaxant to prevent further seizures and by the second day I was sometimes awake. It was truly terrifying to be locked inside my body, unable to talk or move, aware of my surroundings but not able to tell anyone. At night, when I woke, I could see a shape sitting next to me, a figure dressed in white. I believed it was Michael and that he had stayed with me, knowing I would be afraid. I felt a peaceful presence whenever I saw the person clothed in white. When the doctors finally removed all the tubes I tried to speak, but my throat was sore and my mouth felt strange because I had bitten my tongue during the seizure and it was swollen.

A week later I was awake and coherent and was finally told what had happened to me. I asked Michael about my time in the intensive-care unit and the person in white.

'Were you here each night in a white t-shirt?' I said.

'No, Schatzi, I wasn't,' he replied.

Every time I spoke I could see tears in his eyes, and I couldn't understand why. I didn't realize that I had nearly died, or that he was told I would be brain-damaged. His tears expressed his joy and relief that I was able to talk and even argue, because I insisted that he had been there each night dressed in white. He assured me the nurses had made him leave each evening telling him he needed to get some rest. I still didn't believe him and said that someone *must* have been there through the night. I felt them comfort me each time I woke and the fear I felt left me. It gave me the fight to live. Curious, Michael went to investigate and asked if anyone had stayed, but the staff informed him that no visitors were allowed in the intensive-care unit at night. They were adamant that I'd had no one with me and said that on that unit all the medical team wore green or blue uniforms, no one wore white.

I believe to this day that God sent an angel to watch over me.

Losing Self and Home

A week later I was discharged from hospital. I was far from fully recovered and the next six months were a blur. I survived the fit, but I had changed and my ability to concentrate or hold a lengthy, coherent conversation had gone. I also developed a stutter and had no energy to look after our daughter. I struggled to remember how to do the simplest of tasks. It was mentally difficult to make a cup of tea, let alone make up a baby's bottle. Every step had to be written down because I couldn't remember what to do first. My husband had to do everything, even bathe me, as I became forgetful and anxious. He and my mother took over the running of our home and looked after Chloe while I sat in a dismal stupor, waiting for *me* to return.

Every week I attended hospital for tests and monitoring. Each consultant kept saying that I was a 'very lucky girl' and that I 'should have died'. But I didn't feel lucky. I knew God had kept me alive, but I wasn't sure what for, as I was not the person Michael had married. It was a horrible time, but Michael was just happy to have me home no matter what shape I was in. He still loved me, but I didn't feel the same any more. I wasn't sure who I was and felt as though I had left my mind behind at the hospital.

Then, out of the blue once again, my father turned up at my mother's house. It was another unannounced visit from Jamaica, and Mom called to say that he wanted to see me. I laughed at that, as I did not want to see him. I had lost myself to eclampsia but a part of me still knew how I felt about him. I didn't want him to meet my husband, as when I was younger he had condemned inter-racial relationships, and I certainly didn't want him around my daughter. I imagined him contaminating the precious new bundle I had given birth to, just as he had contaminated me with his violence and hate. I told my mother that I didn't want to see him — not now, not ever — and put the phone down in the knowledge that *I* had closed the door on him this time. Even after all this time I still carried the hurt, and could not let it go.

When Chloe was around six months old we went to Germany to introduce her to her grandparents. Michael hadn't told them about the severity of what had happened to me, so they were a little shocked when they saw me. I was considerably altered from the young woman that they had met previously. I had put on weight, and was quiet and sullen. His father, being a minister, prayed for us. Although I didn't experience an instantaneous healing, the day he prayed I felt my thought processes begin to realign. The fog that covered my mind lifted and I could think clearly again. I could enjoy my little girl and the life came back into my eyes. We returned to England optimistic about the future, and were looking forward to a peaceful Christmas. It had been a tough start to our marriage but we hoped that the worst was over.

That first night back home we were both happy for the first time in a long while. After we unpacked and got Chloe settled in for the evening, I opened the post. We had been away a few weeks and there was a considerable pile of letters awaiting us. One by one I opened them, until halfway through something I read made my heart sink. I handed the letter to Michael, and he read aloud the words *'Notice of Eviction.'*

I couldn't believe it. What did it mean? After we had read the letter through, we understood that our friend had rented the flat to us illegally. He was a tenant and therefore we were technically squatters. As I didn't have a job we had been struggling financially and had applied for housing benefit, which alerted the housing association to our friend's illegal sub-let. We were very naive to say the least, and when he had offered us the flat we didn't fully understand what he had done. To us he was a brother in Christ who kindly offered us a place to stay and his integrity was not something we had ever questioned. We had been through what we felt was the worst – I had nearly died. After seven months I was only just getting back my health, and we had gone away in the hope that it would help me to get better, which it did. But this was not news we expected to hear upon our return.

I cried as Michael prayed, and we both sat up that night holding each other, unsure what would become of us. I was scared the bailiffs would throw us out immediately, so the next day we went to the housing association and tried to explain that we didn't know what our friend had done. We asked them to let us take on the tenancy, as we had a baby, and it was just before Christmas, but they said no. The best they could do was give us until the first week of January, but we would have to be out by then. We were left on our own to try to find a place a week before Christmas, with a baby, one income from casual work and no deposit for another apartment.

There was no room at my mother's house, so in the end our only option was to go to the council and declare ourselves homeless, as we couldn't afford to rent elsewhere. The council offices were to close for Christmas, so we had to wait until the new year to see if we could get a place. We spent the holiday packing our belongings into boxes, not knowing where we would live. Chloe's first ever Christmas was a quiet, sombre affair as we could little afford to indulge. My mother helped us out where she could, but we did not want to be a burden to her. It is a sobering thing to get a letter saying you are a squatter about to be evicted and another informing you that you are classed as homeless. The honeymoon period was over.

When the first week of January came we still had nowhere to go. When the council offices reopened we were offered a place in a very rough part of the city. It was a notoriously violent drug haven, and I couldn't believe life had come to this. Where was the happy ending? Why did it only seem to happen in the Bible or fairytales? Where was the romance, and the blessings? I felt cursed and blamed myself for passing on the curse to my husband too, but Michael's optimism was astonishing. He fasted and prayed without ceasing and believed God would find us a good home; we just had to trust him. I knew then why God had placed me with him. He had the determination and tenacity that I lacked.

We declined the council's first offer and were told that we had two more options and would have to accept one, no matter what. I felt depressed but Michael refused to give up and, in-between shifts at work, he searched for a place to live. Meanwhile our finances hit rock bottom – being a casual worker, Michael only got paid for the hours he worked. He had of course taken a lot of time off while I was ill, and most of our savings had been used to keep us going. The little money we had soon ran out and at one point, after getting what we needed for Chloe, we only had ten pounds a week to buy food. It was a lesson in cooking on the cheap: I learned fifty ways to cook tinned tuna, and had a new respect and understanding for my mother's recipes. The ingenuity of necessity that I begrudged as a child came to good use in those lean years.

Yet all the while I felt riddled with guilt as I was still not fit for work and it seemed to me that the only thing I brought to the marriage was ill-health. One morning, as I sat amongst the boxes, we had an impromptu visit from our pastor. He arrived just before Michael left for work and when he saw all the boxes he asked if we were moving. His question made the pent-up tension that I had been holding on to burst out in the form of tears, and Michael reluctantly told him that we were being evicted. As I went to make some tea he told the pastor the whole sorry saga. The pastor assured us that he would do everything he could to help, though I didn't think that there was much he could do.

A couple of days later the pastor called. Somehow he had managed to find another family who were keen to do a house swap with us. Although we would not get a choice in where we lived, he assured us that it was safer than what had been offered. Neither of us had been there before, but that day we drove to the housing office and were given keys to our new home, sight unseen. It was in a town we didn't even know. It all happened very quickly but by the end of the week we had moved into a two-bedroom, third-floor flat in a tower block. Friends from church, Bible college and family all chipped in with second-hand furniture and carpeting and gave out of the little that they had. It was a real lesson in giving and receiving, and their generosity was amazing. Our council flat wasn't perfect but it was home – and it was ours.

We were still relative newlyweds but our vows had already been tested on all fronts: in sickness, for poorer and for worse. I started to desire the health, richer and better times that they mentioned and felt saddened by the way my husband's life seemed to be turning out after marrying me. Everything had changed; the honeymoon period was definitely over. I was a wife and mother but the traumatic events we had been through affected my personality. Michael says he has had many different wives all wrapped up in one bundle in me. The talkative, expressive woman that I was when I got married started to revert back into the shy child again. I was still open to love and friendship, but I was also open to depression. I had come through some tough times: rejection, abuse, isolation and then near death through eclampsia. I now found myself suffering from postnatal depression, which was an added blow.

A New Song

He put a new song in my mouth, a hymn of praise to our God.
Many will see and fear the LORD and put their trust in him.

Psalm 40:3

The eclampsia and depression had lasting effects and took their toll on my confidence. During my time at college I had sung at many churches as a soloist and they still called, asking me to come and sing, but I couldn't do it. The depression made me nervous to the point of being sick whenever I had to stand up in front of people alone. Eventually, our church started a choir and I joined, hoping that singing as part of a group would help me. Although nervous in front of others, I sang freely at home and once again it became my passion, my expression and my escape. However, I didn't want to fantasize, dream or pretend to be anyone else. In fact, I couldn't. I had changed so much that those things no longer appealed to me. Instead, I cried out to God in song.

One day, when I felt so lost and in such a dark place, I told God that I couldn't heal my broken heart but I knew that he could. He had done it before, and I asked him to do it again. I couldn't guide myself through the darkness that I felt but, knowing he was the Light of the World (John

8:12), I asked him to guide me. As I cried, I sang, and before I knew it the melody of a new song came to my mind. The song I wrote that day was called 'God Can' and it became my belief, my prayer, my hope, and it comforted me when the depression was at its worst.

> God can, throughout your test and trials,
> And when your heart is breaking,
> He'll hear you when you call.
> He's here through every situation,
> Your trials and temptations.
> He'll hold you close,
> For I know he's real,
> I know that God can.
>
> *'God Can' by C.L. Schlitter, © 1999 C.L. Schlitter, JoClo Family Music*

This was my prayer every day and it helped me to believe that God could heal me – and he did, for one day the darkness lifted. The freedom I felt was unbelievable and a whole new 'me' emerged. From that point when churches called asking me to sing I started to say yes, as I realized that the story of how God kept me from dying was powerful. It was only when I fully grasped the overcoming power of testimony, that I finally overcame my nerves. I found it was more important to share about the journey I had out of the depression rather than worry about people looking at me. I was amazed by the stories I heard from others as I sang at women's meetings around the country. Many people had been through similar things, and my story encouraged them that they too could hold on to God and get better. Pretty soon we were inundated with phone calls from churches asking me to come and sing.

Michael had always believed in me, even when I doubted myself. So much so, that he initiated my first solo recording project, which was a CD containing just four hymns. He knew I would never do it myself, so by faith he scraped together enough money for us to record with an amazing jazz pianist, an elder from the church. We recorded it in the back bedroom at the home of a local worship leader that we knew. I designed the front cover, which had just a single red rose on it, and Michael burned copies on our battered old computer that someone had given to us. The CD was entitled *A Taste of Things to Come*, as it was my hope that one day I would record 'God Can' on a full album. It was a true learning experience, and we trusted in God to provide the money to enable us to make more CDs, as each time I sang we sold out. He always provided, and eventually we had our own little cottage industry in our tiny council flat, with our little girl Chloe as honorary part-time employee sticking on the labels. This was the beginning of my journey into the recording side of the gospel music industry. It was a very humble beginning.

The leaves had truly fallen and the coat of depression had been removed. I was bare, naked before the Lord – a bundle of emotions, thoughts, ideas, songs and poetry. I wrote prolifically and there wasn't a day that a new song, chorus or poem didn't come to mind. I felt as though I was a new person: not the Claudette of my childhood, shy and introvert, but one who was confident in the love that surrounded her. Michael believed in me and encouraged my singing and songwriting. Chloe inspired me with every new step she took. The youthful days of spring and summer were over and it felt as though the autumn season of change was coming to an end. Things were finally looking up. However, I should have known winter was coming. Maybe I could have prepared for it, but I didn't. I just wanted to enjoy the season I was in.

Winter

Tears

Tears are all I have,
The undercurrents of my dormant emotions
    are trickling down my face.
I taste the salt, I taste the pain,
Tears are all I have.

People ask and mutter,
They fawn and stutter, not sure what to say.
I won't cry to them, no.
Yet tears are all I have.

All other reactions fade,
I can emote no other way,
Tears are all I know,
Easy, fluid, soothing, washing – through
    them I grieve.

Each tear speaks:
Drip – 'sorry', Drop – 'I miss you', Pour –
    'why?' River – 'come back'.
River of tears speak for me,
Tell the world how I feel, for words are
    inadequate for the loss I feel.

Tears are all I have,
I wish I could stop them but when I do
    something darker rules.
Anger, hate and fear all lie in wait, hiding,
    cowering in anticipation.
They are as afraid of me as I of them.
Yet tears are the victor, they wash, soothe
    and balm.

Tears are all I have,
So I let them flow, I let them flow.
Take this river and wash me clean
For tears are all I know.

These tears become my friend,
They do not judge, they don't pretend.
They hold my thoughts, they hold my deeds,
    in every drop you'll see a need
These tears are all I have.

They speak and say 'Goodbye',
Farewell, adieu, however said, I still lose you.
And all I gain is hurt, I hurt again — I fear
    this time will never end
For these tears are all I have.

16

A Season of Singing

Flowers appear on the earth; the season of singing has come, the cooing of doves is heard in our land.

Song of Solomon 2:12

After nearly three years of marriage I started to yearn for another baby. When I first mentioned the idea to Michael, he looked at me in horror. He still had vivid memories of the seizure and of my time in intensive care, and didn't want to go through that again. Our consultant had told us that if we were to have any more children there would be a one in four chance that I could have eclampsia again and that I could die. He recommended that we didn't have any more, but I never wanted Chloe to be an only child. Being a half-sister to everyone, I wanted my own child to have a full brother or sister and it soon became something that played on my mind day and night. It took a lot of persuading to convince Michael that I would be alright, and he needed time to think about it. One day when reading the Bible he saw that children are a blessing from the Lord (see Ps. 127:3–5) and he acknowledged his own desire for a brother or sister for Chloe. After many discussions and much prayer we soon agreed to try for another baby.

Not long afterwards I became pregnant, which was news that was welcomed but secretly made me worry. I held on to the scripture that Michael had read, but one day when he was at work and Chloe was taking her afternoon nap, I was alone in the kitchen cleaning and a wave of anxiety came over me. What had I done? Was I mad? The doctor said that I could die! I began to think about what had happened last time and the predicted likelihood that it would happen again. I felt foolish for even believing that it was safe to have another baby and I started to cry. My selfish desire could well result in my death, leaving my daughter without a mother and Michael as a single father. Why, oh why, had I persuaded him to go along with me? I worried that even if I did make it I would go through an exhausting three-day labour as before. Would I be able to breastfeed? I had been robbed of that with Chloe. I also feared the depression that had been so dark and terrible.

Before I knew it I was having a panic attack and felt as though I couldn't breathe. I held on to the sink for support as the fear took hold. As I did I noticed my Bible on the kitchen table, and in my distress I sat down and opened it to search for comfort. Now, I am not one of those people who use their Bible to tell their fortune, picking out a random scripture, but as I opened my Bible that day it fell open naturally at Isaiah 66, and this is some of what I read:

> 'Before she goes into labour, she gives birth; before the pains come
> upon her, she delivers a son . . . Do I bring to the moment of birth

and not give delivery?' says the LORD. 'Do I close up the womb
when I bring to delivery?' says your God.

Isaiah 66:7,9

My heart leaped when I read the words, 'Do I close up the
womb when I bring to delivery?' In that chapter God
answered every question and doubt I had: he told me the
child would nurse, and that the labour would be over before
it had begun, and I believed that I was to have a son. As I
read it, the panic attack left and never came back, and from
that day on at every singing engagement, concert or conference, I sang and spoke about the word God had given me
about my child. Even when things appeared to be going
wrong, I still held on to the promises in Isaiah 66.

Forgive, Seventy Times Seven

Michael's career was steadily improving and he now worked
for an airline. One week they sent him to America for training and while he was away the pregnancy developed com-
plications. I was taken into hospital, although thankfully it
was not the hospital that had left me lying in casualty for
hours. Chloe, then 3 years old, went to my mother's. Even
though Michael was away he was ready to come back at a
moment's notice, but I believed I was in no danger.

My dislike of hospitals was intense, and I soon found
that dislike was turning into loathing. I held on to my faith
in Isaiah 66, however, and told everyone, even the hospital
staff, that I would be fine. But the test results showed

otherwise. I was pre-eclamptic at twenty-eight weeks pregnant, so they inserted a needle into one of my arteries. The pain was excruciating, but I refused to believe that God would allow the same thing to happen again. He had given me his word that it wouldn't be like before so I knew I was in no danger. However I was mistrusting of the medical profession after the way I had been treated last time and had little faith in their abilities.

Alone but not lonely, I kept occupied by reading and writing. It was nearly ten years since my father had refused to visit me in hospital, and at night I would dream of that time. As the days went by I couldn't shake the feeling that God was trying to tell me something. One morning, when I was talking with other expectant mothers in the cafeteria area, I was startled when two hands covered my eyes. I quickly asked who it was. A man with a thick Brummie accent spoke laughingly and said, 'It's your dad.'

I knew who it was. It wasn't my real father, and I felt a bit annoyed at the flippant use of the term by someone else. It was a pastor I knew and he sat down and encouraged me for half an hour. It was a nice visit, but as he left I was having an inner argument on the presumptuous use of the term 'Dad' by a minister and how insensitive it was in light of what had happened to me. I was not unique, as he would call himself 'Dad' to lots of young people in the church. I'm also pretty sure he didn't understand the issues for me attached to the word but that, in itself, was a lesson. Afterwards, I heard that inner voice challenge my thinking. God had sent me a father-figure but it wasn't enough; I was still bitter and couldn't accept the kindness that was being offered because of the emotional hurt I still felt. I had not forgiven my father.

I was shocked into realizing that everything was different this time around, apart from me. God had reassured me that the labour and delivery was going to be fine, I was being looked after in hospital and a 'father' had visited me. But my heart remained the same. I knew that if my own father turned up again, as he had done when Chloe was little, I would have refused to see him. God wanted me to forgive and so he had gently challenged me by sending someone who unwittingly stepped on my past. The only reason I was annoyed was because I still hadn't fully forgiven my father. I also needed to consciously forgive the staff at the previous hospital for their mistreatment of me, as my bitterness was affecting the way I dealt with the staff at this new hospital. Although difficult, I had to let go of my grievance.

I used that week in hospital to take time to pray and forgive. I forgave the minister for using the title 'Dad' and later wrote a note to him thanking him for his visit, trying to explain its spiritual significance, but I think my message got lost in translation. Jesus told his disciples to forgive seventy times seven (Matt. 18:22, NKJV) and I had to do that, because after my note the pastor referred to himself as my dad even more. Yet I could see God at work because each time he said it I was reminded to forgive my own father. Eventually as the years went by, I even found myself calling the pastor 'Dad' too.

I was sent home from hospital the following week with a different perspective in my heart. I had no idea that healing the heart would be such a long process, yet I understood that just as one gradually weans and introduces a child to new food, God was slowly introducing me to a deeper love.

Whoosh! Here Comes Josh

I managed to carry the pregnancy to thirty-eight weeks, when it was finally decided that I should be induced. By this time Michael was home so we sent Chloe to my mother's, returned to hospital, were booked into a lovely room and waited for our new arrival.

Michael and I were surprised to see Sista turn up in the labour ward. She had remained a dear friend to me and I had asked her to step in if my husband wasn't there at the crucial time, if he was in the States. Somehow that had got misinterpreted and she came for the labour, and neither of us had the heart to tell her to go. She had been very supportive whilst Michael was away, so we said nothing, and together the three of us waited as the induction process began. I was told to walk around and be active, which I did, but when I was examined four hours later the labour had not begun. I have to confess that I began to doubt and became distressed. Michael, Sista and I prayed. The midwife told me that induction usually meant a long labour, but I told her that God said it would be different this time. I would not be in labour for three days and I wouldn't have another fit. To say that she thought I was mad would be an understatement, and a medical team were on standby in case I had another eclamptic fit.

Another dose of medication was given and again I went for a long walk. Four hours later I had no contractions, only mild discomfort, and it looked as though the midwife was right. I was disappointed, as I truly believed the scripture that God had given me, that before I had labour pains I would give birth to my son. The general consensus by the medical team was that it was going to be a long haul.

I was offered a soothing bath to try to relax, as I became anxious, but no sooner had I settled into the bath than I felt a shot. It was as though someone had set off a firework in my stomach. It wasn't painful, just shocking, but it was enough to tell me that the baby was coming. It didn't feel like contractions or the labour pains I'd had with Chloe; it was like nothing I'd ever felt before. I told the midwife but she didn't believe me.

'Now Claudette, you've just got yourself worked up that's all, there's no way the baby's coming yet,' she said patronizingly. She had only just checked me minutes before and said I was not dilated enough to give birth.

Then another firework went off and I gave Michael a look that said 'get me out of here'. We both knew something was happening, but could not convince the midwife and she began a long monologue, explaining how many years she had been doing the job. She knew that I couldn't be ready and tried to persuade me to stay in the bath and relax. Michael politely but very firmly insisted I be taken out of the bath, as in his words, 'She's not the kind of woman to have her baby in water.' (If you know about black women and their hair, you know why.) I got out of the bath, walked around the corner to the room and was bent over with the pressure I felt bearing on me. Yet the midwife continued undeterred . . .

'Now Claudette, just keep calm and get up onto the bed, and I'll check how far you've dilated. I've been doing this for many years now, and I know what I'm talking about. Try not to be upset or disappointed, but I think you'll find that you'll be here until . . .'

I placed one knee on the bed to pull myself up, and before she could finish what she was saying we heard an almighty 'Whoosh!' The midwife shouted for help but before anyone else could arrive the baby's head shot out and the rest of his body quickly followed. She had to catch him mid-flow and the 'Oh my goodness!' she exclaimed was something that secretly gave me a great deal of satisfaction. She could not believe it, and even though I had doubted at one point, God had fulfilled his promise. As I tried to mount the bed, I had not felt a contraction before I gave birth to my son: he was born in a moment, before the birth pains came upon me. I had no pain, no trauma, and even though the consultant insisted I stay in hospital for six days and keep in my cannula (the intravenous needle in my vein) 'just in case' emergency treatment had to be given, I had no problems. I was able to nurse the baby successfully and did so for six months. Everything was different, including me, and I knew that if my father did show up he would be welcomed.

Joshua Michael Schlitter ran his way into the world on Saturday 19 August 2000, and he has been running ever since. The same energy that was in his birth is in his personality, and he is a tornado of liveliness, jokes and sport – his exuberance cannot be contained. He has the sharpest wit and lights up each day with his smile; he is the image of his father.

"Before she goes into labour, she gives birth; before the pains come upon her, she delivers a son . . .' That's exactly what God told me, and that's exactly what happened.

Mixed Blessings

With two children and no recurrence of illness or depression I embraced life with a new motivation. I wanted to be the kind of mother who encouraged her children and taught them to never give up on their dreams, even when they failed. With this in mind I decided to face one of the failures that had bothered me as a teenager. When Joshua was a year old and Chloe was 4, I tried to get some of the certificates that I had missed out on school. I was 30 years old but needed to prove to myself that I could do it and erase the memories of my past. I was no longer a scared child running away and living in a fantasy land, so I went back to college and studied GCSE English and Maths, and passed both.

In English I was awarded a high A* and was flabbergasted when a letter of commendation from the principal of the college arrived on my doorstep. It said that I had been placed in the top five in the whole of England, out of more than 16,000 students that year. The local newspaper even came and took my photograph and did an article on me. It was amazing, as although I had graduated from Bible college with distinction this meant so much more. I had finally passed the school exams that bullying had stolen from me. And not only did I pass, but I excelled. God was truly turning my life around and was making me 'the head, not the tail' (Deut. 28:13). I also took driving lessons and passed my test first time. This gave me the confidence to apply for a part-time job – and I got it.

It all felt wonderful and I was fit and well apart from one thing – my weight. Over the years I had ballooned and at this time I was nearly 19 stone (about 120 kg). I can't say it didn't bother me, but I tried not to think about it. Michael assured me that he still loved me no matter what size I was, and after the difficulties we had encountered when having our children he was just content that we were able to enjoy family life.

At first I liked my new job but sadly, once again, I met with difficulties. There were certain colleagues who didn't like me at all, although I tried to be friendly, and I couldn't understand why. Now when I look back I believe there was a racist element to their behaviour, and it was a tough thing to go through. They fabricated stories about me to my then absent manager, who, without evidence, proceeded to discipline me. It knocked out of me the little confidence I had gained and I wept bitterly at their maliciousness. However, it proved to be a mixed blessing. The treatment I received sparked a chain of events that proved God works all things together for good, for those who love him (Rom. 8:28). At the same time as things got worse for me they got better for Michael, and he was appointed to a post in an IT company. It meant I could resign from my job, as financially we would be better off. I could have disproved the lies that had been told about me but I didn't want to fight any more, not for something I didn't really want. It gave me the push I needed to pursue what I wanted to do full-time as a profession – I wanted to sing.

When a new music director was appointed for the church, he called me and asked me to join the main worship team. I was in the choir and led worship at our inner-city Birmingham branch, but had never done so in a main service. For a while I became one of the worship leaders in church. Previously, I had not been part of the main team as I had been told my voice was deemed unsuitable and wouldn't fit in.

Life always seemed to throw obstacles my way whenever it came to singing but Michael, undeterred, believed that I should also sing as a soloist. We decided I should make my first full album, which was a huge leap of faith for both of us. Unable to find a label to take me on, we had to fund the project ourselves, so we approached the church to see if we could obtain support and financial backing. In return, we offered them all the money from the sales of the CDs. For us it was not about making money, we just wanted to make music. Our offer was declined, and we accepted that, but were disappointed when it was said to the church the same weekend, 'We support people that we believe in', and the CD of a young Christian rock band that the church had paid for was shown to the congregation. Although we believed that God would provide the money, we were saddened and it reminded me of when I was 18 and the congregation was told not to applaud me. Yet, I knew that just as God had turned that around he could do the same again.

By faith we recorded my debut album, *Hardest of Times*. It charted the journey we had walked, and I chose to cover songs that demonstrated God's sustaining power through difficult times. I was still not yet confident enough to believe that my own compositions were worthy of going on an album – my songs were my diary, my inner thoughts and woes. However, when I showed the studio team the title track, which was a song that I had written, they loved it. They asked me to bring in more of my own material. I was stunned that they liked it. I doubted anyone would really like my compositions enough to buy a whole CD full of them. Timidly, I handed over a song at a time and we worked on them, and amongst the songs was 'God Can'. I was very emotional on the day of recording it, crying between every line sung, and at one point we even had to stop recording. I couldn't believe that I was in a real recording studio, singing a song I had written in my kitchen; a song that had walked with me through depression and had given me hope throughout my second pregnancy.

We released the album and to my surprise people loved it, although I was nervous about the songs I had written. I needn't have been afraid, however, because soon 'God Can' became a favourite for many people. Consequently, it became my signature tune and everywhere I went I was asked to sing it. It spoke to people about their own situations and we marvelled at the response. It did so well that we were finally offered a record deal and the album was distributed around the world. That meant radio play, television appearances, features in magazines and engagements where I briefly encountered some well-known names. It was mind-boggling, as I was just a mother of two living in a council flat who really didn't think she had much to offer.

I will never forget the first time I heard my song on the radio. Michael was away in Germany and I was leading worship in a branch of our church. The Birmingham outreach reminded me of my days teaching at Sunday school; we had few instruments but a lot of heart. It was always late by the time I picked up the children from my mother's and headed back home, and one Sunday night as I drove I listened to the radio. The gospel show of our local BBC radio station was on and halfway home I screamed in shock as I heard my song, 'Hardest of Times'. Chloe shouted, 'Yippee!' and Josh laughed. He was only 2 years old and didn't understand that it was Mommy on the radio, but Chloe did, and we both giggled and sang along. When we got home I emailed Michael and by email he too screamed his joy. It was a real night to remember as I just couldn't believe that someone like me could get on the radio. After all I had been through in my life it was a precious moment, which showed me that God was again turning my life around.

After that my songs were played on Christian radio stations around the world and we had enquiries from all over the country. Singing engagements came pouring in and it became my full-time job. I was a professional singer, earning my income from my music. I had made the right decision to finally follow my dream, and it was a truly remarkable time in our lives.

High Hat

In his spare time Michael became my manager, organizing engagements, gigs and liaising with churches and conferences. It was a life-changing experience and sometimes glamorous, yet we still lived in a small council flat. The property market was booming and even though we were better off, we couldn't afford to buy a house of our own. When I was inside our tiny apartment I felt safe and at home, but outside the door was a different story. One by one our neighbours, who were young couples with small children just like us, moved out and got houses of their own. As the years passed by the tenants alternated between drug addicts, wife beaters and gangs of criminals doing deals in the car park or foyer. It was becoming dangerous to live in our tower and I came to dread what my children would see on the short journey up the stairs to our flat. Urine-soaked lifts were the norm and blood spatters were seen regularly on the stairwell. I yearned for a house with our own entrance, where we didn't have to witness anything illegal or violent. It was something of a mission field and we tried to share our faith with our neighbours, but it was a dangerous place to live. My overwhelming desire was to have a garden where the children could play and feel safe and, most importantly, *be* safe.

It was another mixed blessing because despite this one thing life was good, and for the first time in my life I was truly able to say so. I was no longer the bullied child or the rejected or disowned daughter – I was now wife, mother and friend. The protective coats of the past had been thrown off. It was wonderful. The children brought me so much joy. After the birth of Joshua there was no recurrence of post-natal depression and I could enjoy my children completely. I loved every minute of my life, apart from where we were living. Then, one day Michael came home from work and said that he wanted to take us for a drive. He drove to a newly built housing estate in our area, and there before us stood a beautiful three-bedroom house with two and a half bathrooms, a fitted kitchen, a dining room, and it had what I desired most – a large garden. As I peered through the windows he said what I was dreading he would say.

'I want to buy one of these houses.'

'Are you mad? This is far beyond what we can afford. "Don't put your hat where your hand can't reach",' I said, quoting an old saying in my richest Jamaican patois.

Michael was aiming for something far beyond our status, but just like the firm belief I had concerning the birth of our son, he was not to be dissuaded. I tried to point out to him that we had invested what little money we had into making the album and had no deposit for a large fancy house. Like a dutiful wife, I reminded him of the things we lacked. Yet the same man who had believed that a black woman he hardly knew should be his wife was proved right once again. By the new year God had blessed the singing so much that we had enough money to put down a deposit on our dream house. We then saw that it was all part of God's plan that we had been refused financial backing, and had led to us being able to buy our dream house. After seven increasingly difficult years of living in the flat we had a beautiful, brand new home with all the modern conveniences, a garden, and most importantly our own front door, which we didn't have to share with drug addicts and criminals. It was still in the same area, for we had grown to love the area and the people there, but to finally have a home that we could truly call our own was such a blessing. Michael had placed his hat on the highest peg, and reached it. And I never quoted that saying to him again.

Life Lessons

I was in my early thirties, yet I felt like a child, experiencing new things through the joy of my family, a gospel-singing career and our new home. We moved into the house when Chloe was 7 and Joshua was 4 years old, and I learned even more about the Father's love in those years by watching my children. Michael had to work long shifts – twelve hours at a time, day or night. The time that the children had with him was sometimes short and at times they felt starved of his presence. The day shift was particularly hard on them, for unless they woke up early or stayed up late they didn't get to see him at all. They would make all attempts to catch him and would get upset if they didn't see him. Sometimes nearly two days could pass without them seeing their daddy, although he had seen them. He had kissed them when they were asleep, though they were unaware of it. Although he was not present physically, they still felt his love and never once felt that he didn't care. And they were so secure in his love that their reunions with Michael were a sight to behold.

When they finally caught sight of him after a couple of days of missing him, both literally and emotionally, there were squeals of joy. Before he got a chance to fully open the front door he would be besieged by our two little ones. Even though he was tired and hungry after a long day's work, he always had time for them and would play, getting them overexcited, much to my disapproval (especially at bedtime). When he sat down for his evening meal they would flutter around him, twittering and chirping like little chicks – 'Daddy, this happened', 'You know what, Dad?' and 'Look what I can do' – and he was patience personified. Yes, he probably wanted to shut the door and have peace and quiet, but his love for his children far outweighed any desire for solitude. He had missed them too. I saw the Father's love in the earthly actions of my husband.

God is never too tired and always has time for me, and although at times I thought he wasn't there, he still loved me and he still cared. He is my Father. But it was a life lesson that I would forget as time went by. No one could snatch me out of God's hands, but I could certainly try to walk away.

17
The Settling Frost

Anxiety in the heart of man causes depression . . .

Proverbs 12:25 (NKJV)

It was quite overwhelming to see large posters and banners with my face and name emblazoned across them at churches or halls, instead of a wall of graffiti displaying insults. Even at church I was now sought after to lead worship, sing solos and accompany the leadership on events and missions. Going from the person nobody wants to know to being the 'golden girl' of the moment was a strange experience. Some people might have shunned the new acceptance that I'd found, particularly when it came from those who had previously not really bothered with me. But after years of not being wanted, the traces of the bullied schoolgirl still remained. Instead of buying sweets to win favour, I became a people-pleaser, trying to please everyone, eager to sing at church. I especially wanted to please the father figures I had found. Yet my motivation was fear. I was still afraid they would reject me again, so whenever I was asked, I always said yes.

Although I wasn't famous by today's global media standards, even gospel singing in Britain brings its own kind of fame, and I thought it might all go to my head, but I actually found I

struggled with being the centre of attention. I didn't like looking at large images of myself and I felt that it was not at all 'me',
especially with the amount of weight I had gained after having
the children. I was desperate to lose it, so I decided to go on a
diet that was based on meal replacements instead of eating
normal meals. The problem was that the longer I stayed on the
diet, the more aware I became of my weight. After a year of
dieting I had lost more than seven stone, but instead of being
happy I became increasingly dissatisfied. One day I went to
visit my diet counsellor to inform her that I no longer wanted
to continue. I was content at this weight, but what she said in
response to my declaration seemed to fire into my brain like a
bullet from a gun, shot from the past.

'But Claudette, according to your BMI [body mass index]
you're still *fat*.'

She emphasized the word *fat* a few times and then tried to
give a scientific explanation but all the while kept using the
word. It dredged up so many awful memories for me. I went
home and when I looked in the mirror I couldn't help but
repeat the word 'fat' in my head. When Michael came in from
work I told him about it and he assured me that I was perfectly fine and that she was wrong, but I felt that I must still
be carrying too much weight for her to say what she said.

I started to look inward.

Altered Friendship

Sista and I had attended the same church for many years
and were in the church choir together, but I no longer sang

with the gospel choir where we first met or went to the home group that she had been running. The busier I became with singing, the more I needed my evenings to spend time with the children, especially as Michael did shift work. I also stopped going to the gospel choir and her house group for other reasons. From the time I got married my relationship with Sista altered. This was only natural, but once she even told me that she was jealous and over the years at times her behaviour was inappropriate. However, I always looked beyond the occasions when she overstepped the mark, remembering that she had been my first real friend. Along with that, over a period of time a culture of gossip and criticism developed, with Sista seeming to be the main protagonist. Although I didn't want to take part I was drawn in as I clung on to my friendship with her. Michael wanted me to pull away, as the once healthy friendship had become quite claustrophobic and was affecting our marriage, but I initially refused. Loyalty was everything, even if things had changed.

Then one weekend I was singing at a leadership conference in Ireland and a message was preached about letting go of unhealthy friendships and gossip. The night before the meeting I had confessed to Sandie and another friend about the struggle I was having in my relationship with Sista. These two friends were witness to my confession and to the subsequent sermon, and with nudges from both of them as I sat in the meeting I knew things had to change. The sermon confirmed everything Michael had said. Husbands and wives notoriously never listen to each other, and when I got home Michael graciously resisted the urge to say 'I told you so', even though it was written all over his face. I still wanted to be Sista's friend, but after hearing the sermon, whenever our conversations veered off-course into gossip I told her I could no longer take part, as I felt convicted. This added to the gradual breakdown of our friendship and culminated in a complete separation, through what I saw as a hurtful act.

Sista's 'womanism' and its emphasis on perfection, using the Proverbs 31 passage on the 'Wife of Noble Character' as a guide, became a list of prerequisites for Christian womanhood, even down to the way women dressed. This list was taken to its extreme when, at one of her home group meetings, Sista 'corrected' a friend of mine by criticizing what she was wearing (and this was done in front of others). The result of the public correction was that the person was humiliated. Embarrassed and hurt, she fell into a pit of depression and the results were devastating. When I found out about it I called my friend and she met me for lunch, but let me know that she didn't want to see anyone associated with Sista and her kind of Christianity again, including me.

Later, when I spoke to Sista, she defended her actions by saying that God had told her to do it. That was hard for me to argue against, especially when previously God had told her to be my friend, and that had enabled me to trust and consequently find the love of my life. Instead I decided to question the results of her actions, which had destroyed friendships, hurt someone deeply and didn't seem to display what the Bible teaches about loving one another and showing compassion (see for example Eph. 4:30–32).

Nevertheless, she insisted that she was right, saying I was too young to understand and not as spiritually mature as her. Except I was no longer 18; I was in my early thirties and I understood it perfectly – the love had gone from 'woman-ism'. Operating in spiritual gifts had taken precedence over caring for the heart. I didn't know it at the time, but that conversation would be life-changing, as the once beautiful bond between us, that I thought could never be broken, was severed.

In truth, Sista and I had both changed, but I felt the blame lay with me. For years I wasn't able to tell her how I truly felt about her behaviour. If I was a true friend, surely I should have been able to tell her when she was wrong? Still, I felt I owed her a lot and didn't feel I was in a position to challenge her. I didn't want to hurt someone who, in the past, had been so kind to me. However, we were now different people, with different interests and had little in common. The ethos of self-empowerment was no longer something I wanted to be associated with, especially if it hurt the vulnerable.

Bullying Revisited

It was shortly after the breakdown of my relationship with Sista that worship band rehearsals started to remind me of my days at school. Sista, who was also in the choir, would stare at me non-stop throughout rehearsals and her friends would do the same. When they were gazing I would hold my head down or turn around just so I didn't have to watch them watching me. I wanted to speak to them about it but it seemed ridiculous to ask someone to stop looking at me, even though it felt intimidating. Convinced it was all in my mind, I thought I was being paranoid until others noticed and asked me about it. I was satisfied that I wasn't going crazy but I still couldn't confront Sista. Every time we spoke she was polite to my face, yet whenever we rehearsed the intense staring resumed.

I was away a lot, singing in one place or another, but whenever I could I went to rehearsals. Previously I had loved them, but I started to dread them. When I was asked where I'd been, snide comments would be made by certain choir members about my singing ambitions. I tried to shake it off and decided not to talk about it to anyone again. Then one day, in passing conversation, someone mentioned a part of my history to me almost as if it were common knowledge. They knew I had been abused. I listened to them talk and my eyes widened in shock. There were only two people in the church that knew the story of my childhood and the incidents that had occurred: Sista and Michael. I knew that my husband would never have discussed it with anyone and when I thought about the alternative, I was shattered. Then someone else warned me directly not to tell Sista my personal information; they spoke to Michael and me privately, cautioning us to watch our backs. It was like something out of a soap opera; I couldn't believe that it was happening, and in church.

I felt ashamed, as I didn't know how much people knew about me, although of course it shouldn't have mattered. I am a new creation in Christ Jesus and others dragging up my past shouldn't have had any hold over me – nor should their jibes or criticisms – but it did. It hurt and felt as though my name was plastered across the red-brick wall again. In my mind the bullying was being revisited, but this time it was subtle, with gossip and innuendo. Eventually it proved too much and I didn't want to hear the stories being told. They perpetuated the spreading of malicious gossip and I wanted no part of it. Even when others tried to goad me into finding out, I refused to listen because it would only have served to destroy me further. I went into denial, refusing to believe that Sista could have been to blame.

I started to think that maybe I deserved the treatment I was getting, maybe I had abandoned her and therefore that justified the criticism. Michael told me it wasn't true, but I couldn't help but blame myself. Ever my hero, he wanted to challenge the apparent source of the gossip, but I begged him not to. We had no evidence, no proof and, no matter what, I still loved her. I believed that the problem must have been me. I must have been on the wrong path and that was why she had turned against me. No matter how much Michael tried to persuade me otherwise, I firmly believed that I was at fault. I had been rejected so many times, and it seemed to me that when I finally stepped out on my own things started to go wrong, so it must have been my fault.

Yet I knew I couldn't react the same way I had as a child: I couldn't fight and I couldn't hate; I couldn't get tough because I had been soft and vulnerable for too many years. So I found myself unsure of how to react. I tried to forgive, yet it hurt so badly. I didn't know what protective coats to put on and so instead I got frostbite and withdrew. I retreated into myself, finding that my nerves returned when I performed and that I felt sick when I was the centre of attention. Because of what the diet counsellor had said I also worried about my appearance and felt obese.

Winter had begun, and just as I was trying to deal with the loss of friendship and conflicting emotions about my weight, I heard a sudden 'ping'.

Sickness and Death

One Saturday evening as I was getting the children ready for bed I did the most innocent thing in the world – I blew my nose. I had suffered from chronic catarrh for years but had recently found myself having cold after cold. Blowing my nose was no big deal, but as I blew, my ears blocked and a ringing noise began in my left ear. The next day in church I felt quite ill and the noise in my ear got louder. I couldn't even raise my head without it spinning. My ears ached with the vibration of the music and the two symptoms combined made me dizzy and nauseous. It continued for about a week but I soldiered on until, reluctantly, after I had lost all sense of balance, I went to see a doctor. The GP said that I had labyrinthitis (inflammation of the inner ear due to an ear infection) and that it would be better in a couple of weeks.

Knowing that it was only something minor, when another week passed and my gums started to swell I made little of it. I was not too concerned as I had experienced problems with wisdom teeth before and was sure it was nothing to worry about. Nonetheless, weeks later I was no better, in spite of antibiotics and various tablets, so finally Michael took action, knowing I wouldn't. Believing that the problems in my ears and gums were connected somehow, he called the dentist. During my appointment my mouth was X-rayed. I still was not at all concerned when I was referred to the hospital. The dentist had seen a calcium deposit in my jaw and said it was probably nothing but wanted to get a second opinion. The following week Michael and I attended our local hospital where yet another X-ray was taken. As I left the X-ray department we became separated because I had used the wrong exit. So when I was called in to see the consultant to discuss my X-ray I was on my own.

I walked into the room and when I saw the look on the nurse's face I was quite unnerved. Something was wrong and although she was obviously trying to hide the worry on her face, when she smiled it was a 'tell' like no other. I suspected something had gone awry but supposed it to be some kind of administrative mishap and that my files were missing, which had happened before. I sat down casually as the consultant asked me to look at my X-rays and, using his pen as a pointer, he motioned in circles around a cloudy mass on the screen. When he said that they had found a lump I thought, 'What's the big deal?' I wasn't being brave, I just thought my dentist had got it right and it was just a deposit. But the look on the consultant's face wasn't one of someone who was going to tell me that I had too much calcium. I watched his mouth move as he said the tumour had changed and was eating my jaw. My first thought was, 'Hold up, you didn't call it a lump – you called it a tumour!'

He carried on talking for a while but all I heard was the odd word: 'Tumour . . . CT scan . . . cancerous . . . operate . . . '

I couldn't believe my ears, it was all too confusing. I had gone to hospital to look at something relatively minor and now they were using words such as cancer and talking of surgery. I interrupted the doctor and asked the nurse if she could find my husband. She nodded sympathetically and rushed out of the room to get him. When Michael came in everything was repeated to him in detail. The magnitude of what was being said hit us both and he grabbed my hand. I squeezed his to make sure I wasn't dreaming. He knew that I wasn't taking it in, or that I was in denial, because I whispered to him repeatedly, 'All I've got is an ear infection, that's all. It's just my wisdom teeth playing up.' The consultant spoke earnestly with care and concern, and I appreciated that, but I really didn't listen to him. I just kept thinking that it could not be happening. Not after everything we had already been through. It seemed so unfair. Hadn't I been through enough already? What lesson hadn't I learned yet? My friends had turned on me, and my weight was starting to bother me again, but this? This was too much. We held hands as Michael was given details of the scan I was to have. Then the consultant told us to prepare for the worst and explained the worst-case scenario. While he was pointing at the screen he illustrated what he would have to do, and it was then that the full impact of what he was saying hit me.

'We will probably have to remove your lower left jaw and replace it with a piece of rib bone, reconstructing your face. It is quite a major operation, and the best we can hope for is that we can remove the lump without losing most of the jaw, but we won't know that until we know what we're dealing with. That's why we need to do a CT scan straight away. Just try to stay positive.'

'But I sing!' I exclaimed, 'I use my mouth for my living. I'm a gospel singer.'

His face saddened when he heard that, and he tried to reassure me that he would do everything possible so that I could still sing, but as the tumour was sitting on an important nerve there was a risk that I would lose some movement in my face. I couldn't believe it. After years of struggle and rejection finally I was a singer – what I'd always wanted to be – yet cruelly, it seemed like it was all being taken away. We left the hospital and our hands never parted. I couldn't talk and cried all the way to the car. A tsunami of tears overwhelmed me and I don't think Michael said anything either; if he did, I didn't hear him.

We went straight to church to see our pastor and he prayed for us, yet I said to him that I didn't feel I could take any more. This was the last straw, and I would break. He assured me that I wouldn't, but he had no idea how hard life had been and how fragile I felt. I felt that all my strength was gone and my faith was too small. It was all too much. Michael, his eyes moist with tears, turned to me and said, 'Don't worry, I have enough faith for the both of us.' And he meant it, for only he could know how much I was crumbling inside.

As we were leaving the church office I received a text message and then the tears turned to bawling. My old school friend, Angel, who had been suffering with cancer, had died that very morning. We had kept in touch over the years and I had called her when I found out she was ill and promised to visit. Sadly, that day, the very day I had planned to go to see her, I had my hospital appointment. And she died. Whilst I was crying over the lump that had been found in my jaw she had passed away and I never got the chance to say goodbye. I felt guilty for wallowing in self-pity when I should have been visiting her instead. Once again I began to look inward, into myself and my actions, and found them wanting.

That Sunday in church I told Sista about the lumps and her reaction was the final nail in the coffin for our friendship. 'I knew you'd come back to me, I knew you'd need me.' I shook my head and told her that I was letting her know because she was my friend, but by then it was too late. She said other things, but her first words revealed her heart. It wasn't about me; it was about her and her need to be needed. From then on she became an acquaintance and nothing more.

The combination of all these things proved too much. The next day, whilst Michael was at work and the children were at school, I went to the shops. I bought large bags of cookies, cakes, crisps and other junk food and I ate them all. I had an almighty binge and I felt so guilty afterwards that I determined to stick to my supplement diet religiously. I didn't realize that I was about to be reacquainted with my old enemy . . .

The cycle of guilt and blame had returned.

Winter Takes Hold

Owing to my pending operation I stepped down from the worship team at church and cut down on all singing engagements. Michael and I had been married for ten years and, although we still loved each other, the busyness of life had taken away our true focus. We had to get back to the heart of our marriage – us – and this was a real wake-up call. As I have already said, the journey of our relationship and marriage is another story, but we needed to find each other again in order to face the challenge ahead.

In the following weeks I had a CT scan and then we had to wait for the results. Waiting can be exciting, especially when we are waiting for a birthday or a holiday. Sometimes it can be boring. But this, this wait was agonizing. When the results finally came we found that the tumour was benign, and we were relieved. However, I was not out of the woods yet. When I heard that it was benign I foolishly thought that meant I was fine, but I was to find out that 'benign' does not necessarily mean that it isn't harmful. I had a rare condition called gigantiform cementoma, which causes tumours or cysts in the bones of its sufferers. My upper and lower jaws were full of lumps and whilst most were inactive, one was growing, causing malformations in my jaw, infections and the pain I was suffering.

I must admit that when I first heard about the condition I really didn't understand what it was, or the full implications. I certainly didn't realize it meant I was facing more surgery for the rest of my life. At first, they only wanted to remove the lump that was eating my jaw. I would lose some jawbone and teeth but not everything. It was disturbing to hear that, if left untreated, the tumour would eat away at the jaw until it disintegrated, but at that time I believed I would need only one operation. I employed the same blocking techniques I had used as a child and tried not to think about it. At church everyone concentrated on the good news that it wasn't cancerous. I ignored all the others things the consultant said and continued making my second album in the belief that I would soon be well enough to continue.

As I was an independent artist, Michael and I had committed ourselves to the project financially, so in spite of all these things, a couple of days after I found out about the tumours I was back in the studio. Once again, song became my prayer life and I wrote 'When U Praise', trying to encourage myself and not give up hope that God would heal me. I also wrote a song called 'I'll Be There' about God being my friend when others let you down. It was a real diary of what I was going through, but all the while my health was deteriorating. We managed to complete the recording and one month after we launched the CD in concert, I had the operation. They removed the tumour but also found a smaller cyst for which I had to await laboratory results. My jaw was reshaped as it had expanded, and all went well apart from certain after-effects of the surgery.

Whilst in the recovery room I had what an anaesthetist later told us was a flashback. Due to the cocktail of drugs I had been given I experienced post-traumatic stress-type imagery of my earlier fit and my body went into shock. It was so bad that at one point Michael was even called to the recovery room, and it was only when he told them what had happened to me after the birth of our daughter that they understood how the sudden attack had happened. Years later, when I was having further surgery, we found out from the specialist that this was known to occur in such cases, and he changed the type of medication I was given in order to prevent it happening again.

It took six weeks for me to recover from surgery, although thankfully they had managed to avoid the nerve. The other cyst they found was also benign but after the operation the ringing in my ears continued for months and caused severe migraines. Nightmares of the fit began to haunt me and I would dream that I was trapped in my body, unable to move. When I awoke I would feel as though I were suffocating. I was referred to more specialists and endured more tests. This was the beginning of a journey of poor health that I didn't know would affect not only my vocation but also my ability to walk.

Michael and I started to struggle financially, as we had invested in the second album but had to cancel engagements due to my poor health. It was a hard time and I found it particularly difficult when people told me to 'have faith' or 'hold on'. I found myself laughing, as it was all I could do to stay sane.

In what seemed like a short period of time I had encountered malicious gossip, loss of friendships and poor health, and the end result was that I felt cold inside again. Nothing seemed to prepare me for winter, and everyone, including me, thought I would be singing again in no time. What I didn't know was that my next singing engagement would be the last time I would sing in public for five years. Winter crept up on me, and it was a bitterly cold time – but things were about to turn arctic and I had no idea how cold I would become.

18
Bleak Mid-Winter

The spirit of a man will sustain him in sickness, but who can bear a broken spirit?

Proverbs 18:14 (NKJV)

It was Sunday morning, just six weeks after surgery. The phone rang and Chloe ran to answer it. It was my mother. I thought she was calling to see how I was doing. She had been a tower of strength whilst I was ill, and I believed it was just one of her routine calls. I was slowly beginning to look like myself again after the swelling had gone down and felt well enough to go to church, so I had got up early to do my hair. I was jiggling and wriggling to music in front of the mirror when I took the phone from Chloe and heard my mother speak in a dazed tone.

'Your brother is dead – Indie's dead.'

The words knocked me off my feet, and I dropped the phone, collapsing in a heap on the floor as though someone had punched me. I was stunned. Chloe shouted for her father and he ran upstairs and took the phone.

On Saturday 21 July 2007 my eldest brother Indie died suddenly in his bathroom, for no apparent reason. At the time they could find no cause for his death. This was the final straw, the thing that finally caused me to break. When winter had finally taken hold, I had no protective coats. I crumbled.

That morning as we arrived at my mother's house we were greeted with a scene of dumbstruck grief. The house contained the eerie silence of a family gathering where one of the members is not only missing but will never return; where everyone functions but falls at the same time, tripping up on their words while offering copious amounts of tea to strangers who offer their condolences. It was only when the house was still and we sat together, all the family members bar one, that we knew our family had forever altered. To me, life had lost all point and purpose. It broke my heart to lose Indie and to watch the grief that encompassed our family. His death devastated my mother. She was overwhelmed with sorrow – we all were. We heard later at the inquest that he had undiagnosed diabetes and had gone into a coma, and we wept bitterly knowing that a simple blood test could have prevented his early death. He was only 52 years old.

Although I haven't mentioned him in this book as much as other people that is not because he wasn't part of my life. Indie was part of the fabric of my existence, part of my past and my childhood – the good part. He was my big brother. He was family. After being diagnosed with a rare condition and having surgery, with possibly more to come, I really wanted life to resume as normal. I didn't think it was much to ask for, but losing him meant that life would never be the same again.

I may not have seen my brother regularly, but when I did it was like going back to the days of my childhood that were happy. The last time I had seen him was about two months before his death. He was at my mother's house, taking her old sofa away for her. He carried it single-handedly, as he was a fit, strong man. I arrived just as he had finished, and when I got out of my car I shouted to him, 'Father Abraham!' I used to call him that as a joke because in the last few years Indie had come to some kind of understanding in his faith and had changed his ways. He no longer drank or smoked, and for some bewildering reason had grown a magnificent beard that, to me at least, resembled a biblical patriarch; I would tease him over it, and pull at it playfully. My last memory of being with him was that I ran up to him, as if a little girl again, and we hugged as usual. It was so normal, but so special. He was the one brother that I could still hug. Troy and I, although friendly, were never close again after the years of silence, and although I had a loving relationship with my brother Art, he was not a 'huggy bunny', as I would say. Indie was. I would *always* get a bear hug from him and I will treasure that last hug. If I had known it was to be our last, I would have held on to him forever. We talked for about ten minutes and then he was gone, off on his way.

The next time I saw him he was laid in his coffin, wearing that awful make-up they put on bodies to try to make them look like their previously alive selves. It is impossible, for the spirit is gone, and they never look the same. Indie was part of my life, my history, and I loved him dearly. When he died, my heart broke. Still in recovery from surgery, and with the remains of stitches in my mouth, I led worship and sang what was to be my last song for a long time at his funeral. It was a CeCe Winans song called 'He's Concerned', a powerful ballad about God caring for us in our grief. I had to believe that the words were true, and that God was concerned about me, but tears were all I had.

I thought I had dressed for winter until it came.

I Quit

When winter finally came I had thrown off my self-protective coats, but I didn't have the coats God had for me either. In my grief I refused to be comforted. I wouldn't let the Father dress me in his love as he wanted to, and as I threw off my old coverings I threw off God's too. I wanted to be left alone in my grief. I grieved over Indie and held on to my sorrow and pain. I also grieved over my health, my life, my past, my lost friendship with Sista and my singing career. I was so tired of fighting all the time. Life had been an uphill struggle and I felt I couldn't take any more. Self-pity became a friend and depression a constant companion, and I kept their company more times than I ought.

At first I refused to sing, but later when I tried I started to have anxiety attacks in which it felt as though I were dying. This happened especially in church where I believed everyone knew about my sordid past. So I gave up and gave in. I quit singing and I quit life. I went back to office work and flitted from job to job, hiding my gospel singing history as I just wanted to forget it all. I didn't really want to do office work and even though I was highly trained and experienced I took jobs that were demeaning and soul-destroying – but it was what I felt I deserved. I didn't think I could do any better or that I should ever try to make a better life for myself again. It always ended in disaster, so why try? The jobs brought in the extra income that we needed as we were struggling to meet our day-to-day bills, with the responsibility of a mortgage and two young children. While I worked illness plagued me and I suffered constant colds, infections and viruses. I put up with them all, believing I deserved it because of my selfish ambition in trying to be a gospel singer. Michael wanted me to seek help but I refused because of my experiences in the past. I just wanted to be left alone.

I was miserable and resorted to the coping mechanism of comfort eating, which soon heralded the return of bulimia. You may imagine my surprise at being faced with it again aged 35. During my childhood it was a very secret battle, but it was hard to maintain that secrecy as a mother and wife. I had children of my own, and hiding it from a soon-to-be teenage daughter proved increasingly difficult. I didn't want her to be like me or find out what I was doing. Realizing how it was affecting my children and my husband, I went to seek guidance from the church. They tried to help, but sadly the things they said actually made the situation worse. At one point I was made to stand up and turn around to be examined. Upon inspection I was proclaimed 'alright' and they could see nothing for me to worry about. Not only was it humiliating but it confirmed my opinion that I was being judged by the way I looked. Each day the battle got worse as I binged and vomited in order to maintain my weight, and to punish myself for the rotten person I believed myself to be. I would try to hide it from Michael, but he knew. Every time I did it, he knew. He could see that something was desperately wrong, although when he tried to talk to me about it I became defensive and moody.

I began to think that I didn't need singing, writing, poetry or any of the creative things that I had previously enjoyed and I stopped doing them all. It was foolish of me, as I needed singing and creativity almost as much as I needed the air I breathed. They were the way I communicated to God, and when I decided to stop singing – even at home – well, I stopped praying. I stopped speaking to God and, although I was going to church, I was vexed. I was mad at him for allowing Indie to die and had broken my friendship with him just as one would break friends with schoolmates. The problem with breaking friends with God is that you lose all spiritual sustenance and joy. The joy of the Lord is our strength and that makes *him* our strength (Neh. 8:10). I had no strength to help me carry on. It was I who had closed the door on God yet I believed that he had left me. I looked back at my life and all I could see was misery, trouble, hardship, poverty and heartache. Yes, I'd had glimpses of joy and happiness, but I focused on all the bad things. I was miserable; I didn't want to admit it but I was lost without him.

It felt as though I had lost everything and everyone. I still had friends but eventually I pulled away from them, and in less than six months after Indie had died I was suffering from severe depression. I no longer had the mood swings I'd had as a young woman – I was permanently depressed.

Then I decided that I no longer wanted to go to church, for I could see no point in going: I could neither praise nor

pray; I could not sing. Every time I walked into the building I felt nauseous and dizzy. The crowds, noise and music
would cause anxiety to rise within me until I could hardly
function. I wondered whether the physical symptoms were
caused by my being so far from God – that must be why I
couldn't bear to be in his house. I even wondered if I was
going insane. The ringing in my ears became a constant
companion and the music in church aggravated it to the
point where I would have to arrive after the worship and
leave before they began playing again. One Sunday morning as Michael got ready for church I told him that I wasn't
going and I'd never be going back. There was a look on his
face that said, 'I'm losing her' – and he was right, because
by then I had decided that I no longer wanted to live. I
loved my children and my husband but I truly believed I
brought nothing good to them. I thought the best thing
that I could do for them would be to leave them, and I plot-
ted my demise.

One morning I collected all the tablets that were in the
house and stretched them out on the bed. I told myself that
if I took them it could all be over and the many years I had
wasted trying to be something I was not (a Christian) would
end. I thought it would be the best way to end it all, but
changed my mind when I realized that Chloe would have
been the first one to find me when she came home from
school. I couldn't do that her, so I went for a drive. While I
was travelling along a dual carriageway I managed to get my
car to more than seventy miles an hour, which was a lot for
my tiny little engine. I hoped to close my eyes and let it
crash so everyone would think I had been killed in an acci-

dent. About to carry out my plan, I panicked and slammed on the brakes when another car came along. I wish I could say that the thought of my family stopped me from committing suicide, but it didn't. It actually made it worse since I thought I had brought them nothing but sorrow and that they would be better off without me. What prevented me was the other car that I saw. As much as I wanted to take my own life I would have hated to take someone else's, which is what I would have done if I hadn't stopped.

A Glimmer of Hope

I went home and binged and made myself vomit once again, which was by now a daily routine. Later that evening, in my despair, I confessed all to Michael. Our marriage had been under great strain since Indie's death and he had tried to help me with the bulimia, but it was hard. Having tried church and not getting much help, we were at a loss as to what to do or who to talk to. Knowing I would refuse medical intervention, Michael searched the Internet for information and it was there he found the Anorexia and Bulimia Care (ABC) website. It was a Christian charity for eating disorder sufferers and their families. He wasn't sure if they could help but in desperation he called the support line, and my journey of recovery began. In just one conversation the advice he received gave him a glimmer of hope. They recommended literature for him to read to help him understand eating disorders and advised him on the best course of action. They also sent him their magazine, *Lifeline*. By this time our marriage was at breaking point, as for nearly a year I had resorted to the behaviour of my youth. I had binged, purged, self-harmed, starved, dieted, and got so depressed that I could no longer function as a mother and a wife. I stopped doing any of the things that brought me or my family pleasure and sank into an abyss that nearly destroyed us.

When Michael first mentioned ABC to me I wanted nothing to do with them and rejected any contact. I didn't even want to read the magazine because I thought no one could help. My shrewd husband left the *Lifeline* magazines on our bookshelf in plain view at my eye-level, however, and one day I started to read them secretly. It may sound hard to believe but it was the first time I had heard stories just like mine. I had felt ashamed of being bulimic again because of my age. I was in my mid-thirties and thought that these things only happened to teenage girls, but *Lifeline* featured people like me, who found they were still suffering after many years.

I desperately wanted to be free from the mental torture of an eating disorder, so I finally agreed to speak to someone from ABC and Michael arranged for them to call me. I spoke to a lady who was kind; she did not condemn or criticize, but she understood and shared her own experience, and for the first time I realized I was not alone. I too was left with a glimmer of hope that I could get better. Through email correspondence with ABC and reading the recommended books and the *Lifeline* magazine I finally plucked up the courage to go to the doctor and told her what I was doing. I was prescribed antidepressants, and I have to say that at first I felt wretched for having to take them. I hated myself, and even felt that my husband had failed me, as he had been unable to help me. You can see how far my mind had descended into depression by this time. It took a long time for us to figure out that I was suffering from depression and it was the cause of much of the stress and strain on our relationship. Once it was diagnosed, however, Michael then understood what he was dealing with.

Our experience showed us that mental illness is still poorly dealt with, especially in churches where the emphasis is on healing, victory and promises. The issues are mentioned, prayed for and preached about, but the hard work and investment of time, energy, support and care can be sadly lacking. Many churches don't have the resources or the expertise to deal with such issues. This is what Michael found, so after doing his own research and using ABC's advice he instigated the process of recovery that brought me back from the brink. He sought help through the private healthcare he now had, after being promoted in his job.

For a year I had been suffering terrible rashes all over my body which were so itchy that I would scratch until I bled and cried with the pain. Using Michael's healthcare cover I was seen by a specialist and was diagnosed with chronic urticaria, or hives, which can be brought on by stress. The treatment they gave me worked and so we also sought help for my bulimia. I went to a private clinic and received counselling. The recovery took time and involved establishing eating plans, but most importantly I was made to look at the reasons why I resorted to comfort eating. I had to address my feelings. My husband didn't leave my side throughout and used up all his annual leave from work to attend each appointment with me. We fought the battle of bulimia together and at the same time mended our marriage.

My Jonah Years

During that time I continued to work and had even gone back to church. I still believed in God, and tried to hold on to what little faith I had remaining, but it was tiny. In fact, it was minuscule, but it was there all the same. Things had changed. Sista had left the church, and along with her went some of the people who had perpetuated gossip. It was nice to be a member of the congregation instead of a worship leader and even nicer not being a gospel singer. It meant I could take part without any of the pressures or problems that my time in the worship team had brought me.

I had many jobs in what I call my 'Jonah years', where, although I was recovering from bulimia I was sure there was no way that God would ever want me or use me to sing for him again. I was far too weak a Christian. Although I started to sing at home and could frequently be heard humming a tune around the office, I was convinced I would never be a gospel singer again. Well-meaning colleagues tried to persuade me to audition for television talent shows, but I wouldn't. I still remembered the day in 1988 when I heard the singer at the evangelistic event and what it was like to sing for God, and if I couldn't do that then I really didn't want to sing at all. So I decided to put all my energy into finding a new career.

For a couple of years I took job after job, trying to find something that I liked, but never did. In fact, in all the jobs I'd had since quitting singing, there wasn't a single one where something didn't happen to make me mistrust people more. From societies to churches, I tried working for them all, and some of the treatment I witnessed was nothing short of outrageous. Fed up with scheming and malicious people, I always chose to quit rather than persevere. From moody, erratic managers, to scheming, spiteful colleagues, I'd seen them all, and was often sickened by the vanity and materialism that surrounded me. Yet although I had become cynical, at each place there was a golden nugget, or I formed a friendship that long outlasted my time there. Everywhere I went God reached out to me. Though I tried to run away from him, he was calling to me through individuals who were truly Christ-like and caring, even if I couldn't see it.

My final place of work was very different to any that I had ever worked at before. The way I got the job was nothing short of miraculous, as at first I didn't even make the shortlist. However, I now believe God wanted me there, not just because the job was good for me but because I had to learn to trust again. I had been badly hurt and I wasn't sure who to trust any more. Church, friends and even family had let me down and I had become jaded. My philosophy was to expect the worst of people, then I wouldn't be disappointed. It was a pleasant surprise when I started my new job to find that I had a kind and considerate manager and was with a team that was supportive and friendly. I doubted it could last but they proved me wrong. I grew to love them and I threw myself into my new job with gusto. I had finally found a job that I enjoyed and was working in the community with families and children. I hoped I could work there until retirement and never have to sing again. But I was doing a Jonah, and running in the opposite direction to where God wanted me. However, the whale that was to swallow me up and put me back on track was on its way.

The Great I Am

After a year had passed I was finally settled; I was in recovery from depression and bulimia, with a restored marriage, thriving children and a good job. The only problem I had was my health; I still struggled but always tried to keep working. Then one morning at work I was looking at the computer and the screen became blurred, so I wiped it to check it was clean, but no matter how much I cleaned it I couldn't see it properly. It took a few minutes for me to realize that the problem wasn't the screen but my eyes. Soon the room started to spin and I nearly collapsed on the floor. I had been feeling ill for a long time, and always carried on regardless, but this time I could hardly walk, so a colleague took me to the doctors where once again I was told that I had labyrinthitis. The doctor said that I was to go home and rest and I would be recovered in two to three weeks.

Ha!

Five weeks later I was still ill and although I tried to go back to work I couldn't walk without support and was being sick constantly. I had recovered from bulimia but was now being sick without forcing myself to do it. I was losing weight, but it was not a good thing on this occasion. I couldn't even do my hair or get dressed without falling. What's the point of looking slim just to topple over? Within days of returning to work I had to stop because I couldn't look at the computer screen without my vision distorting. Then I lost the ability to control eye movement (a condition called nystagmus), which was terrifying. Because of my medical history I dared not surmise what it could have been, but I was so ill that I called for the elders to pray for me as Scripture commands.

Whatever was ailing me was getting progressively worse and I experienced horrifying night terrors. Night after night I would feel the bed spin uncontrollably and would scream with terror. Michael would hold me and tell me that I wasn't falling, but I was sure I was. The walls would move as though they were breathing and when I tried to stand I couldn't figure out where the ground was or whether my feet were touching it. I became progressively worse, until one night, at around three o'clock in the morning as Michael was holding me, he said words that spoke right into my spirit.

'Schatzi, it might feel like you are falling, but you are not. I've got you, I'm holding you. No matter what it feels like, I can tell you now, that the fact and the truth is that *you are not falling, I am holding you.*'

I know that my husband was speaking to me physically in the here and now but it was as if God was talking to me anew. God had my life in his hands, although I thought I had fallen away. I felt that he had abandoned me, but as my husband's words rang in my head the voice of God kept speaking into my spirit: 'I AM HOLDING YOU.'

God was holding me. I might have gone far away from him but he had never let me go. He kept his promise that he would never leave me or forsake me (Heb. 13:5). In every job I'd been in, he had been holding me. Throughout my time of grieving, he had been holding me. Through illness and depression, he was still holding me.

'I AM HOLDING YOU.'

All night I felt God's arms around me as he spoke into my heart. With those words from my husband I heard God's heart tell me that in spite of the way things looked or felt, he had my life in his hands. It felt as though I was falling physically, emotionally, and spiritually, but he was holding me. I then realized that no matter what, his love remained.

Vestibular Neuronitis

My symptoms were severe and with horrendous migraines, and neck and back ache, I was in daily agony. Before long, I became incapacitated, only able to walk assisted or with a walking stick. I was 38 years old and truly Claudette – the name that means 'one who is lame'. I was bedridden for three months. I had MRI scans and I saw neurologists and specialists galore, all to eliminate the possibility of a brain tumour. After they had ruled out anything sinister, eventually we were referred to a balance clinic. The first assessment involved three hours of rigorous tests with all manner of contraptions that made me feel decidedly worse, but at the end I was given a diagnosis and, most importantly, a prognosis.

It was found that I had a balance disorder called vestibular neuronitis, which had been caused by an infection and had done permanent damage to the nerve sensors in my inner ear. My right ear was working at a lower rate than my left, which meant that the signals my brain was getting from the tiny nerve sensors that control my balance weren't working properly. I had suffered 30 per cent damage. To put it in layman's terms, my eyes and my ears stopped speaking to each other. This can cause headaches, face and neck pain, imbalance, forgetfulness, anxiety and depression. The debilitating nature of the condition can be very taxing on the brain, which is trying to deal with a lot of conflicting information at once. It appeared that I had probably suffered from it since the first infection I'd had years before. It might have been the initial cause of my anxiety and depression, which were then compounded by the surgery I had and the loss of my brother.

The most important thing we heard on the day of the assessment was the prognosis. I could and would get better, but it would take rehabilitation and a lot of patience. I was prepared for the first but had none of the latter, as I am notoriously impatient. The specialist I saw called me a 'character' because I was so joyful, but I was joyful not because of what he told us, but because I knew God was with me. The faith which I thought had died was battered and bruised but not destroyed. I held on to it in the months ahead as the intense battle to regain my health began.

A Woman for All Seasons

The Room

Majesty enters the room,
Silence resounds.
As he turns to look at me
I search his face for love.
It is there.
It is mine.
I love him.
He loves me.
I am whole.
And in the room a door appears.
He takes my hand and leads the way.
I will follow,
He will lead.
'It is finished.'
I am loved.

19
The Real Me

Experience: that most brutal of teachers. But you learn, my God do you learn.

C.S. Lewis

Through those years of illness I went through a rebirth of my faith and of myself. I began a quest for the real me, not the bullied child, nor the assaulted teenager, nor the loved wife, devoted mother, betrayed friend, nor even the gospel singer. I wanted to find the real me and be completely free from the thought patterns of my childhood that had managed to resurface in my mid-thirties. Thus I began to seek my healing, not physically, but mentally, spiritually and emotionally. I knew the physical healing would come, but the most important aspects of me that needed healing were my mind, heart and soul. I had neglected them for too long.

The first part of the curative process was the writing of this book. Years previously, when plagued with thoughts of my past, I heard God clearly speak to me, telling me to write it down, and that through it I would find my answers. I did, but I chose to write it as a fictional account of a girl who had been bullied as I had been. After writing just a few pages I wrote no more, as it was too depressing for words and I found it upsetting to write. So I abandoned that project and tried again, this time writing a spiritual reference guide for struggling Christian women such as myself. It was a failure, as I tried to write in a dispassionate and detached style and not include my personal story. I wrote as though I were a minister pontificating on the things of life, which is not me, so after writing many chapters I put it down and wrote no more.

It was only when I experienced failing eyesight and was struggling to walk that I truly began to face my story. Each day at home for months I lay in bed and wrote, taking the notes I still had from my first writings and changing them to the real story, the whole story. What you have read are just individual chapters of my life, as I decided to select specific incidents that help to show how I came to a state of love loss and negative thinking and how God changed my life. I wrote it for me and in it I faced everything (as incredibly a lot more happened that I haven't included here). After I did it I stopped blaming myself. It was a cathartic experience, as I cleansed myself of all the hurt, abuse and pain by handing them over to God. I could see myself for who I was – a frightened, scared little girl who grew up and learned how to accept love from God, her husband, children, family and friends, but not how to accept love from herself. I had never loved myself and that was why, when the most recent hardships came, I fell apart. I did not think that I was worthy of God's love, Michael's love or my children's. I didn't even think I deserved a singing career, so when criticism came I believed what was said instead of having faith that God was in control of my life.

In this process I saw God's love reaching out to me from the age of 5 to the present day and I learned the reason why bulimia was able to resurface later in my life. Mentally I still carried the thought patterns I had inherited from my youth. I had blamed myself for the things that had occurred in my past, but through writing my story I saw that I wasn't to blame for everything. Yes, I was responsible for certain actions and I repented of those, but it was necessary for me to see where my thought patterns came from; by finding their origin, I could change them. I faced them and saw them for what they were, and realized that Jesus had taken all those things from me on the cross – even the sins that others had committed against me. I had to surrender fully not only the hurt but my lack of forgiveness and see myself as God saw me: forgiven and loved, through his grace. It was the greatest discovery that I had ever made, and it led to my final mental and emotional breakthrough with bulimia, knowing that I had to accept the one love I had rejected all my life.

I had to love me.

This meant being real, and I embarked on a daily walk to pursue the truth. It was not a truth concerning what others had done towards me. I didn't go over the past to apportion blame, but to finally acknowledge how I truly felt. When I knew the truth, it set me free (John 8:32). I had to get real in order to give my true feelings to God. For too long I had learned to cover up how I felt with various coping mechanisms. Throughout my childhood I blocked things out using comfort eating, bingeing and purging. In my teenage years I sang my troubles away in a fantasy land of pretence, trying to be someone else. As a young woman I took on board 'womanism' and used positive confession. I proclaimed a future victory, always looking for a better tomorrow, but never appreciating fully the day I was in.

Too often I spoke the Word, but did not truly live and breathe it. I was in a kind of super-spiritual denial as I tried to ignore my fear of failing, my fear of rejection and my fear of fear itself. Even as a married woman, I relied on my husband's strength in a bid not to face my own frailty. My pursuit of truth eventually showed me what was blocking the perfect love of God. Fear had hindered me from letting God clothe me in his love. I had lived in fear of the past. For years, I punished myself because of the choices I had made and I worried that I would make the same mistakes again. Fear of my past hurts and heartaches had caused me to stop singing. Fear of being judged by my weight caused me to diet and led me back to bulimia. Fear reigned. God wanted to place his love inside me, but these things prevented me from accepting that perfect love.

> There is no fear in love. But perfect love drives out fear, because fear has to do with punishment. The one who fears is not made perfect in love.
>
> *1 John 4:18*

I like the saying, 'If you don't know where you are from, how can you know where you are going?' Well, I didn't know where my thinking had come from. The negative thoughts, self-loathing, self-pity and the fears had their origin, and once I had written them down and faced them I realized I no longer had to be the frightened girl who thought no one loved her, or that she was unlovable. I was loved all along.

Love and Grace

Love had been evident throughout my life, but I couldn't see it. I wasn't looking in the right places and had focused on the negative, partly because I was afraid to enjoy the positive. I didn't think I deserved to be happy. However, when I wrote about the joyous Saturday mornings and the times of fun in my childhood, I saw that I *was* loved. I remembered the dear friends I met on my journey and how each time I walked away from God he drew me a little closer towards him. He had guided my steps and he met me in my distress when my father disowned me. Love *was* evident.

When I wrote about the crazy young German, whose unwavering love for a lonely black girl from the inner city knew no bounds, I knew *for sure* I was loved. As I looked at the miracles that occurred when I had my children, who daily give me so much joy and love, I saw God's love. And even in winter, when I tried to shut down and run away from him, God had loved me. Against all odds I was still here and, though physically weak and disabled, I could see that I was loved. From the time Michael told me I wasn't falling, every time I woke up with disorientating dizziness, God comforted me.

One night, something amazing happened. I was dreaming and in the dream was singing:

Through spring, summer, autumn, fall;
Let me be wrapped up inside your arms.
I need you for the reason,
To be there for all seasons.

And when harsh winter bites so cold,

It's the warmth of your love I know.

I love you for the reason,

That you're there for all seasons,

    seasons.

'Seasons' © *2010 C.L. Schlitter, JoClo Family Music*

Waking up in my dizzy state, I grabbed my phone and hobbled to the bathroom with my walking stick and sang the song into the phone to record it. It was four o'clock in the morning and I had just written my first song for years, 'Seasons'. It answered many of the questions I had often asked God about why such sad times had happened in my life.

The song speaks of the way that he had been there for all seasons, even when I was abused, bullied and assaulted. He had cried with me when friends turned against me. He had grieved at my father's behaviour and mourned the loss that I felt. It wasn't that God looked the other way or caused any of these things to happen, or that he didn't choose to protect me. The fact is that we live in a world with trials and tribulations, criminals and their victims. We live in a world that is consumed with the pursuit of self-gratification. I will perhaps never understand some of the the things that I went through in my childhood, but I now understand the love that sent a Son to die, so that these things could be removed from the heart of man (John 3:16). The Christian faith does not give us immunity from the troubles of life but a powerful remedy for both the sins and hurt that life can bring.

For the next few weeks, each night songs would come, and then it started to happen in the daytime. It was as though a dam had burst within me and the music I had buried for three years came flooding out. With each song came an answer to my questions about the truth. It was exhilarating, as never before had I had such a burst of creative energy, even though I was physically ill and weak. Chloe, Josh and Michael would laugh with me and at me as each day I woke up excited, shouting, 'I've got another song!' My then 13-year-old daughter even sweetly patronized me one day, hugging me and saying, 'Mom, you're so cute, you're like a child sometimes.'

I loved that, as it felt as though I was getting back my childhood. Indeed I did feel like a child, seeing things as new for the first time, and I felt wonderfully, amazingly, powerfully and supernaturally loved.

This love I felt caused me to change my focus. When I was bulimic I used to feel guilty if I didn't pray each day and read my Bible. I did so out of a sense of obligation that enslaved me, instead of freeing me. During my illness I noticed that on the bad days when I was physically unable to read or pray, I felt no guilt. That was because I finally accepted that God was my Father and not a distant, austere figure who would punish me for not spending time with him. Our relationship did not end because of my inability to pray, as he was nothing like my earthly father. I was being loved continually. My prayer life changed radically when I finally forgave myself and was no longer afraid that I had messed up far too many times for him to forgive me. He would *always* forgive me.

When, at the age of 15, I had sung 'Amazing Grace' at school, I did not think his grace was amazing. I had been assaulted, threatened with a knife and burnt with cigarettes, and in my pain I could not grasp the message of the hymn. During my journey of discovery I came to appreciate it anew – for the hymn summed up my life story. I had come through many dangers, toils and snares, and grace had brought me safely through. It was grace that drew Jesus to the cross for me. Grace was God's love in action, from the moment I was sent to Sunday school and heard the stories of Jesus. It was grace that continued to teach and prove itself to a doubting, fearful child. It was what drew an Angel of a girl towards me at school and eventually brought me back to the faith I had rejected. Throughout my life grace had indeed been amazing. Grace is the love that forgives, holds, heals and cherishes. Grace is the love that never gave up on me even when I gave up on myself. All the verses of the hymn speak to me, but one in particular illustrates what God's grace had done throughout my life journey in the faith:

> The Lord has promised good to me.
> His word my hope secures.
> He will my shield and portion be,
> As long as life endures.
>
> *'Amazing Grace' by John Newton (1725–1807)*

He had been my shield and portion, and, as hard as life had been, I dare not imagine how it would have been if God's grace hadn't been there keeping me. There are many people who have suffered similar things to me, and much worse, who are not here today because they had no one to turn to.

In their despair they gave up the fight of life. I discovered that even when I despaired, grace kept holding me, and will continue to as long as life endures.

I started to see a different person emerge: not just a new me, but the *real* me came to the fore. She was someone who wasn't afraid to fail, or afraid of rejection. I finally saw fulfilled the love letter from God that my friend Calvin had passed to me nearly twenty years before. God's priority was me and not my work, and he was rebuilding my walls. I saw the wounded daughter, the sick mother, the fearful sister, the betrayed friend and the loved wife for who she was. I saw how God saw me, the *real* me. I had grieved, mourned, tried, failed, hurt and been hurt, but I had learned that throughout it all I was loved by God, and through him I started to love myself.

The Long Road to Recovery

Although I had been suffering from a balance disorder for more than three years it was the final year that was the most debilitating. When I lost the ability to walk or function properly I was classed as disabled and awarded the appropriate welfare benefit for my condition. After my diagnosis and subsequent therapy we had hoped to see an end to the hardships that had plagued our family for so long. Life did get better for me as my health slowly improved and I persevered with my therapy, but it was hard – very hard. There were days when I just didn't want to continue trying to get better as it took too much concentration and effort, with daily walks, eye exercises, and balance and posture exercises. I also needed lots of rest. I learned to live in the day that I was in and not to try and plan too far ahead into the future. I didn't even think about what the future held, in fact, and just hoped to get well enough to be able to walk and maybe even function properly as mother and wife so that I could look after my family again instead of them looking after me.

We worked through the rehabilitation programme together as a family, with Michael ensuring I did my gaze stabilization exercises, Joshua, the sports fanatic, going for daily walks with me, and Chloe, as ever my coach and cheerleader, correcting me in my posture. Together we battled through every exercise until I got to stage two of the rehabilitation programme. I could walk again unassisted and, although slowly, without my walking stick. I still struggled in large venues with conflicting visual information and noises, such as shopping centres, as my eyes were still unable to quickly process busy environments, leaving me disorientated and confused, but generally they were easy to avoid. The one place I really wanted to go but couldn't cope with was church. At first I could only attend for ten minutes and then had to leave as I would fall over. Michael and the children made me feel like a champion athlete with their encouragement, however, and eventually I was able to stay for nearly thirty minutes without being sick or falling.

It was a difficult journey, and each day was a battle. It was hard seeing the looks of pity that my friends sometimes gave me as I shuffled slowly like an elderly person.

Frustratingly, it would take a day to recover from a fifteen-minute walk, but I rejoiced that at least I could do the walk, whereas before I had struggled just to get out of bed.

The illness prevented me from returning to my old ways and I found that I no longer needed escape mechanisms or strategies because I had finally let God dress me in his garments of love. In learning to love myself, I also learnt to love others and open myself up to them without fear of being rejected.

My command is this: Love each other as I have loved you.

John 15:12

Now that you have purified yourselves by obeying the truth so that you have sincere love for each other, love one another deeply, from the heart.

1 Peter 1:22

Love cannot be contained — it must be shared.

In the past, when I had despised my very being it made me judgemental and unforgiving towards others. I couldn't see the good in them because I couldn't see the good in myself. I judged them as harshly as I judged myself, and I have to say that my time of embracing 'womanism' had fuelled that. I then started to focus on the good in me, or I should say, God's love in me: a love that accepted me as I was — sinful, fearful, negative, unforgiving; a love that dealt with the things that I needed to change in a gentle manner, with care and concern. He had not forced that love on me, nor his will, nor had he demanded perfection

before I could talk to him. As I wrote my story I began to
see that God had used me when I was broken, bulimic,
depressed and lonely – in spite of all my failings. I understood that he could use me because he gets the glory when
he chooses the 'foolish things of the world to shame the
wise' and the 'weak things of the world to shame the
strong' (1 Cor. 1:27).

During my time of rehabilitation, almost every week I
saw someone who I could share my story of God's love
with. I was weak, struggling to stand up straight and I
didn't appear victorious outwardly. But I shared with them
the love that God had shown me. I had no prepared
speeches, but spoke from my heart. Some of those people
had made mistakes, just as I had done, and felt unworthy
to pray even in the privacy of their own home, let alone
step into a church. At times I heard stories of suffering far
greater than my own, and I found myself crying over the
loveless state that they were in. I realized that God had
cried even more tears, for us all. I spoke to many individuals who just needed to know that they were loved, people
just like me, and they began their own journey of understanding how much they are valued by God. Some dealt
with issues of unforgiveness in their own lives, others just
needed a hug and to be told that God still loved them. God
taught me to love as he loved me and to care as he cared
for me, with compassion. That was why I had to love
myself, in order to go beyond me and reach out to someone else.

One remarkable consequence of this sharing was that I
was offered a new record deal, even though I was in no fit

shape to sing. Nevertheless, the label believed not just in me but in the testimony that God had given to me. I hadn't sought them out, but God proved how amazing he is, as he created opportunities even when I appeared to be physically useless. It didn't take long for me to say yes, as I already knew what songs I wanted to do. They were the songs that had brought me through winter. The album *Days, Seasons, Times* was born from the trials and dreams I'd had in my time of recovery.

Working on the album motivated me to keep going even though I still had many physical hurdles to overcome. One of the songs I wrote was called 'In the Morning' and for me it was another 'God Can', as I sang it to myself in the worst times and held on to the scripture that says 'joy comes in the morning' (Ps. 30:5, NKJV).

Writing my story enabled me to see how hard the journey had been from my early years to the present day, but now I could also see how much love God had poured my way. He was always watching over me and was ready to guide and love me, if I would let him take control. The key was for me to surrender completely. The biggest obstruction to my healing was me. I was still trying to fight my own battles and I still held on to the remnants of the past that were so integral to my character. I not only had to let go of my own protective coats but I had to completely surrender my whole life to God, and that meant all my fears. When I finally cried to the Lord and asked him to take over and heal me and dress me, he did. Winter had been one long, cold night, but I knew God was promising that the morning would come.

I Am Loved

It was just a dream, final fantasy,

Holding out, giving up what was left of me.

Falling on my knees, desperation leads.

Waking up, getting out, finally I breathe.

And as I close my tearful eyes,

Weeping may endure for the night,

But in the morning . . .

Chorus:

I wake up in the morning and the tears dry up.

You say it's gonna be OK.

I turn it over to you, I surrender all,

And in your arms I will remain.

I wake up in the morning and the sun comes up,

Giving me a brand new day.

And I'm no longer hurting, I don't have to cry,

'Cos joy comes in the morning

'In the Morning' © 2010 C.L. Schlitter, JoClo Family Music

I finally gave myself up to God, all of me, and he accepted me just as I was. It taught me to accept people as they were, just as he did. I didn't have to be perfect, I didn't have to have a plan, a vision, or a ministry, and I didn't even have to be positive about it. I just had to be open to love and reach out to anyone who came my way, and that is what I did. God was refining and working on my character even when I thought he wasn't, for I had spent many a year worrying about the speck in my brother's eye instead of removing the plank that was in my own (see Matt. 7:5).

The complete healing of my mind came at the right time because I didn't know that more tests were to come. The winter wasn't over yet, but I was now clothed in the right garments and with a right mind, and it proved essential. I became a woman for all seasons and, for the first time in my life, with a new understanding of God's love and no fear, I was finally dressed appropriately.

20
I Am Loved

Forgive, and you will be forgiven.

Luke 6:37

We were making headway with my rehabilitation; progress was slow but steady. The inner healing that was taking place had far-reaching results. Day by day, slowly but surely, changes began to occur in me. They were minuscule at first, just little things that I didn't notice but Michael did. First of all, the nightmares stopped. For years I'd had terrible nightmares and would wake screaming. They were of memories from the past that never left me. From the first time I suffered abuse at my father's apartment, to the eclamptic fit in the hospital – I'd had recurring nightmares of them all. During my recovery the dreams stopped and, although I didn't sleep through the night because of dizziness and pain, I was more relaxed and could have a deep, peaceful sleep when I rested my eyes.

Next Michael noticed that certain things didn't bother me in the way they had done before. At times I could be extremely controlling and a perfectionist, teetering on the brink of having an obsessive compulsive disorder. It is that search for perfection that is usually at the centre of the downward spiral of thinking in a bulimia sufferer. In the past, if what I did wasn't perfect, even with such trivial things as cleaning my home, then I thought it was a complete disaster. I criticized and condemned anything I did that was not a complete success. During this time I changed and stopped being my harshest critic. The biggest change in me was the long goodbye to my old companion – fear. It had accompanied me for many years, yet it was a deadly cohort – never giving, always taking. Gradually Michael noticed that I no longer worried about the future and was no longer afraid of the past. All these things changed in me, although I wasn't aware of these changes until my husband pointed them out.

Each day the smile on his face got wider, and I could see that he was happy. The potential that he had seen in me from the beginning was being realized and I was no longer so self-absorbed with my own inner burdens. I came to understand that when I was grieving for my brother and had got lost in depression, Michael had lost his best friend – me. Now I had returned to him and we fell in love anew as he forgave the many times I had rejected his love and assistance. We behaved like love-struck teenagers, much to the consternation of our children. But letting go of fear and embracing love meant I could love my husband and children freely, with a deeper understanding of their value to me, and of my value to them.

I continued to have my faith tested: the tumours in my jaw grew once again and I had to have more surgery. It was hard, but in God I had the strength to carry on and each time I faced an operation I felt his presence ever closer.

A Poorly Timed Call

I was making good progress with my recovery and was about to embark on the recording of my third album. It was a new beginning, but in the midst of it all we received news that we never imagined hearing. Michael's 10-year-old nephew was missing – he had been abducted. It was an unimaginable event, every parent's worst nightmare, and was all too real for us as our son, Josh, was the same age. It was an awful time and it is a tragic story, but it is not my story to tell. This book is about my life and how events have impacted me, so I shall concentrate on the impact the event had on me and my family.

For the first couple of days all we could do was hope and pray that he would be returned unharmed. Michael wanted to go to Germany and see if he could be of any assistance, and I urged him to leave straight away, but he worried about leaving me and the children. I was still disabled and struggling with the day-to-day running of the house. However, the thought of what the family was going through made my situation pale into insignificance. It put all the things going on in my life into perspective, and my focus had to change from my recovery to supporting my husband and looking after our children so that he could be free to go to his family. After the first forty-eight hours had passed we booked a flight for Michael. I assured him that we would all be fine, as I needed him to be confident that he could go.

The disappearance impacted the whole family, including our children. With Michael away Chloe became my carer.

She is the most remarkable teenager and, with the serious responsibility of taking care that I didn't have a fall or an accident, she coped amazingly. Previously I had fallen down the stairs, and almost set fire to the kitchen due to my inability to concentrate, and now Chloe was in charge of making sure that Mom didn't have a dizzy turn.

While my husband was away I decided to contact many of the churches at which I had sung to ask them to pray. I also emailed our friends from Bible college, many of whom were now in the ministry. Friends from around the world got their churches praying, and prayers and messages of support poured in. The body of Christ is truly wonderful when it comes together, and we were encouraged that people from all over the world were praying for the child's safe return.

The encouragement and support that was given was tangible, much needed and wonderful. I focused my energy on prayer and keeping my therapy going so I could look after the children. Then one day I called a minister I knew to give him an update on developments in the search. It turned out to be a poorly timed call that had the potential to set me back in all areas of my recovery. After sharing details of the event, the conversation turned to a subject that at first took me aback. He challenged me about my lack of church attendance. Even though I had been attending and tried to say so, the minister cut across me as I spoke. I tried to be polite and explain that I was registered disabled and had a visual impairment, and was astonished at his response.

'Well, just wear sunglasses.'

I nearly choked laughing and said that my problem was that I needed more light, not less. I was debating in my mind whether to try to explain the intricacies of vestibular neuronitis, when I was unexpectedly rebuked.

'Look, daughter, I'm your dad, and I need to rebuke you. Stop being so stubborn and go to church. Nobody minds if you have to keep getting up. I know you'll accept this from me because it's in love.'

My heart sank when I heard those words and he continued in that way for quite a while, rebuking me and saying things that were quite unpleasant. It reminded me of the conversation I'd had with my own father the day he disowned me; it had the potential to drag up so many hurtful memories. Some of the things he said could have damaged my self-esteem, confidence and trust – and in the past would have done. But this time they didn't – *because God had healed me.*

This was a time of change. I was hurt, I can't deny that, but I was no longer at a loss for what to do. This time I thanked him politely for his prayers and ended the call. Then I talked to my Heavenly Father: I told him how much it hurt and how I felt, and I forgave. God had loved me when I was mad at him for Indie's death and he had waited for me when I turned my back on him in a pit of depression. He had forgiven me for so many things I'd done wrong, and because of that I forgave those who misunderstood me and hurt my feelings. I held on to what was true and noble, and thought of those things (Phil. 4:8) rather than the insensitive words that were said. Not wanting to worry Michael, I didn't tell him about the conversation at the time. Later, when I did, he was angry that someone had used such a difficult time to take a swipe at, in his words, 'my vulnerable, disabled wife'. The phone call had the potential to regurgitate the pain of the past, but it instead marked the day I knew that I was healed.

The past no longer held me captive. I was free.

Forgive, Forgive and Forgive Again

Michael went abroad to visit his family regularly for five long months, each time in the hope that the boy would be returned. After months of waiting, praying and hoping, sadly his nephew's body was found. The murderer was captured, but for all that time we had lived in hope that he would be found alive. It was a shattering conclusion.

Becoming a woman for all seasons meant I had the strength to support my husband in his time of need. Being clothed in God's love and forgiveness meant I did not resort to the patterns of an eating disorder, or crumble and retreat when someone was horrible to me. Instead, I prayed, praised and proclaimed his power to keep us from falling. God kept my family together in spite of overwhelming circumstances, and when Michael needed me, at last, I was there for him. I was no longer the fragile girl that he always had to take care of. I did not have to be supported emotionally by my husband, but as a whole person I could love him completely when he had his inner trials. Michael grieved in his own quiet but intensely deep way. Even though I was physically lame, I was spiritually and emotionally whole and therefore able to look beyond my problems and help others with theirs.

It was a remarkable time of inner healing for me, and during that period I saw a light and compassion that had eluded me in my childhood at school. The love I received from people was truly amazing. My work colleagues had supported me throughout my illness and were truly wonderful through that time. I was supported by people who did not share my faith but shared my heart and, as a consequence, I found that I was able to share my faith with them anyway. The news impacted everyone – friends and family. Everybody that we knew who had heard about Michael's nephew felt the pain of the loss of a young life so needlessly taken. No matter what faith, persuasion, nationality or colour, they all cared, and all showed forgiveness and compassion. God healed deep wounds, and he showed me how intolerance and prejudice can be overcome. It was not a time for being right or wrong, but a time for setting aside firm opinions and accepting each person's way of dealing with a crisis. It taught me to love with the love of Christ as people grieved and tried to make sense of the senseless.

This mood of forgiveness even prompted me one day to call the person who had, in a moment of bad timing, rebuked me regarding my church attendance. I told him that I forgave him and I loved him. He didn't ask me what for, which at first made me wonder if he already knew, but then sadly he said rather arrogantly, 'I should think so – so you should love me.' He didn't respond the way I anticipated and when I thanked him and politely ended the call I was again reminded of my behaviour in the past – of the incident when I was 20 and just about to go off to Bible college, when my father suddenly turned up and

I had cooked his meat but not spoken to him. I believed then that I had done enough and did not have to forgive him since he was unrepentant. As a young woman, my cold response to my father had continued a cycle of revenge and unforgiveness. My father had never once said sorry for his actions, and because I held on to that the past had not let go of me. I walked in the pain of what he had done for many years, even though my life had moved on. But I now finally understood that, just as with the minister who rebuked me, forgiveness wasn't about him – it was about me.

I had a choice to make – either perpetuate the cycle of retribution and bitterness or embrace a life of grace and forgiveness. I chose forgiveness and it released me from bitterness stemming from the time of the abuse, the bullying, and even Sista and my father. The Bible asks me to forgive as I have been forgiven. Sometimes it is not about making a restorative phone call or confronting the person who hurt us. They might not even acknowledge that they caused us pain, which in itself can be hurtful.

Even when trying to deal with my own feelings about my nephew's murder, at first I struggled to believe that the forgiveness of God extended to someone who could perpetrate such a heinous crime. I thought that if ever there was a crime against the Spirit of God, something that was unforgivable, then maybe this was it. Yet I knew that was not the case. The pursuit of truth had finally led me to the reality of forgiveness – it is there for all. The poorly timed phone call taught me that no matter what, my heart had to remain free: free to love and free to forgive.

Months later I was scheduled for yet more extensive surgery on the tumours in my face and a few days before I went under the knife I heard that my father, whom I hadn't seen or spoken to in twenty years, had passed away. I was very surprised at my reaction upon hearing the news that he was dead. I cried.

I didn't just cry, I bawled and I grieved for the man who had rejected me, used me, forced me to witness his violence and portrayed me as his girlfriend. I couldn't understand why I would feel such a sense of loss over a man who, in truth, really didn't care about me. As a child I had loved him, and when I became a teenager I despised him and gave up his name. He had disowned and attacked me, and I had rejected him, refusing his visit when I was a parent myself. For a whole day I tried to make sense of how I felt, as I wept bitterly. Eventually, I cried myself to sleep. When I awoke that evening I told my daughter about his passing and said that I had cried but didn't know why. She looked at me, perplexed, and said, *'But he was your dad.'*

I have amazing children (if I say so myself), for every day I learn from them just as much as they learn from me. In those five words she showed me how far God had brought me. Any hopes of reconciliation with Dad were gone, and I felt cheated. I had cried because he had never heard me sing and would never meet my husband or his grandchildren, and I knew I was partly to blame for that. Unwittingly, my daughter allowed me to acknowledge and own the fact that the man that I had hated was indeed my father, and I loved him. The forgiveness and love that God had placed in my heart ran so deep that I did in fact love my father.

It was as if he had been the best father in the world and not the drunken one that he was. I loved him, and wished that I could have shared the forgiveness that I had found with him. I grieved over his death just as God was crying over his lost soul. God loved him, just as he was, and sent his Son to die for him as well as me. God's love compelled me to love my father. My tears were of regret in not being able to tell him so, and of how much God loved him too. I was free from all bitterness.

> Get rid of all bitterness, rage and anger, brawling and slander, along with every form of malice. Be kind and compassionate to one another, forgiving each other, just as in Christ God forgave you.
>
> *Ephesians 4:31–32*

I didn't get the 'happy ending' to our relationship of which I had often dreamed, but I was happy that when the end did come I was free from the burden of bitterness. My own love proved insufficient, as it was conditional, just as my own forgiveness demanded that the other person be repentant before I could forgive. But because God loved me, I loved my father. I could love no other way as I had proved that I was incapable of loving on my own. Yet I was filled with God's love.

> And I pray that you, being rooted and established in love, may have power, together with all the Lord's holy people, to grasp how wide and long and high and deep is the love of Christ, and to know this love that surpasses knowledge – that you may be filled to the measure of all the fullness of God.
>
> *Ephesians 3:17–19*

Days later when I underwent further surgery they made an incision, cutting open my gum and jaw line, to reshape my jaw. They took a centimetre strip of bone away from the lower left side of my face, sawed at the jaw bone and removed yet another lump – it was the most invasive operation I'd had so far. Enduring more excruciating pain was no picnic, and I would be lying if I said I didn't feel very low at times. I still struggled with the odd wayward thought and the occasional 'down' day, but that was alright, as God showed me that was why he sent Jesus in the first place. He became human so that he could truly understand what it was like to have our fears, our heartache (when he lost his friend Lazarus he cried), our weaknesses and temptations (as when he was tempted in the wilderness). He knew what it was like to have that little devil jumping on your shoulder whispering sweet negatives in your ear. I found that his presence and joy remained with me through each trial, and songs flowed from my heart daily. I had finally allowed God to take over.

I Love Me!

It was a new season and as I looked back at my life I had to smile. I saw all the guises of me, and the women I had wanted to be. When I was a child I wanted to be like Whitney Houston, and then like the evangelist's soloist. When I got older still I tried to present a persona that was what I thought I should be through 'womanism', which was the woman in Proverbs 31. She is there as an ideal but I became enslaved to its ideology. I became a gospel singer and thought I had to portray an image that was just like her: confident, beautiful, immaculately dressed, fit and healthy, calm and collected. The 'Ideal Woman' is trained and skilful; she is talented, resourceful, helpful and decisive. I had some of these qualities but not all, and when I fell short I told myself I was a complete failure. That is why when I was the subject of gossip and negative things were said about me I crumbled, because I wanted to be seen as perfect – there is an element of pride in all of us, and mine was of appearances.

Of course it hurt to have no friends at school and be bullied so cruelly. My innocence was stolen when I was abused and assaulted, and it was soul-destroying to be disowned by my father. It hurt when people betrayed me, and I have been through enough physical pain for a lifetime. Losing my brother threw me into a state of grief that led to utter despair, and I don't deny that my future looked bleak when I was bedridden for months and then had to use a walking stick. But I had never before seen such suffering as the loss of a child brings. I used to think that these things happened because I lacked faith, but I couldn't have been more wrong. God didn't make the hardships happen, but he used each trial as an opportunity to demonstrate his forgiveness and grace. Each hardship enabled me to become the woman I am today: someone who loves no matter what the day, season or time.

I suppose there are a lot of women like me with certain secrets kept hidden in the recesses of their mind, who only bring them out when a private moment comes up with a close friend or in a counselling session. It has been through sharing the secrets in my life with friends in those private moments that I realized that I am not unique in what I have been through, and that if more of us would tell our stories to each other maybe we could help to heal the wounds of the past and move on to embrace the life God has for us. That is why I have finally shared my story. I was 35 when I began to make the journal notes that I had been writing for what felt like an eternity into a book. I suppose you could say I went through a mid-life crisis – and I think I did. It is only in the last few years that I have finally learned about who I am, and I can at last be myself.

When I was younger I would mentally plan what I was going to say, or the mood I'd be in, as I didn't really know how to be myself. I didn't like myself. But I do now. If I were to describe myself I would say that I am a sociable woman who prefers being alone. I am a 'drama queen' – not in the sense that I make a drama out of every little crisis, but I am a storyteller with a big imagination and can spin a yarn or two. I'm a jolly, outgoing person who is also at times melancholy and introverted. One of my strengths is also my biggest weakness: honesty. I am truthful, but sometimes brutally so. I can't stand arguments but I enjoy lively debate. I am confident but at times insecure; noisy but I also love to be quiet. This is the person I am now, and she was probably there from the beginning but I just couldn't love her, and I didn't think others would either – but this is *the* real me.

One of my saddest and happiest days was when I left my last job. The contract had ended but I had not been there much in the final months due to illness. It was the one workplace where I can honestly say I had been myself, as I had come through the other side of my journey of self-discovery. I was sad to go because I had truly enjoyed working there and the team were wonderful, but happy to leave as I was about to record my third album. There was an emotional goodbye. When I read my leaving card I cried. On the front were pictures of the team, including me, and inside along with their handwritten sentiments was an acrostic that read:

C – Cake
L – Laughter
A – Attitude
U – Unforgettable
D – Determined
E – Effervescent
T – Talented
T – Talkative!
E – Elegant

They had no idea of the names I had been called before, but this is what they saw in me. I had been the real me and they liked me for who I was. Instead of being called stubborn, I was called determined. Instead of being called arrogant, I had attitude. To be called effervescent, talented and even elegant was too much, and I cried with joy. It was so beautiful. I was also so glad that the C stood for cake, as I love to bake and my colleagues were often the victims of my experimentations and inventions. Through this God also reminded me of the names he had given to me:

Chosen, Called, Delivered, Healed, Forgiven and *Loved.*

God had renamed me from the day I put my hand up as a child, and he confirmed it when I was older and recommitted myself to him. In fact, each time he had given me the same name – *Beloved.*

> For God so loved the world that he gave his one and only Son, that
> whoever believes in him shall not perish but have eternal life.
>
> *John 3:16*

He gave his Son with a love that reached out to the world even though it didn't want him. He loves me whether I am seeking his love or not. In this knowledge I can honestly say that I love me – all of me: the good and the bad, the silly and the wise, the weak and the strong.

I love me.

I love the way God loves me.

I love the way he loves the imperfect me and accepts me the way I am, and because he accepts me I accept me too and through that I accept others. That is what makes me a loved woman. I am now 40 years old and it has taken me half a lifetime to be able to say 'I love me' and mean it. Michael once said to me that it takes but a second to break a leg but it can take months for it to heal properly. Well, I was once a broken leg that took many years to fully heal. The last few years of sickness, bereavement and depression were just the final part of the process that God began thirty-five years ago when I asked him to be my friend.

One thing that life has taught me to be is a realist. Whilst I can be extremely cynical at times, I am still a person of faith. As you have seen I wasn't (and am not) an *amazing* person of faith. I failed, doubted, feared, ran away and gave up, but I now see what faith really is for me. Faith is the ability to go beyond myself and still say, 'I know whom I have believed, and am convinced that he is able' (2 Tim. 1:12). Or in my own words, 'I know that God is real and he loves me.'

I know it sounds ridiculous and simple but that is what my faith is – ridiculously simple.

It is about trust.

Trust is one of the hardest lessons that I have had to learn through the seasons and I am still learning. My story isn't one of a life that is totally victorious or dismally defeated, but it is one of trust. It is one of faith. It is one of reality. It is one of love. Now life is about one – me, living for the One – God, and reaching out to one – you.

So, can I ask you, reader, a few questions? Do you know that you are loved and do you know *who* loves you? If you don't then please know that the same God who has been with me for the whole of my life is there for you too. God has been there in each season of my life, whether I was aware of him or not. I am now in another season, but now I am like Joseph, dressed in the King's garments of love and righteousness, and he calls me Beloved. I know I didn't get the ultimate happy ending like Joseph did: my father died and we didn't reunite. And I haven't been healed physically (yet). But when I look through the Bible I see there are a lot of people like me who didn't see their happy ending either, yet they were called people of faith (Heb. 11:13). The same faith they had gives me strength for each day and hope for tomorrow. It comforts, consoles, hugs and loves. It is love from the One who sent his Son to die for you on a cross and is still reaching out to you today. If there is one thing that I would like to pass on to you about my story, it is this: God loves you.

So, now as the seasons turn again, I come back to the question I asked myself at the start of this book: *How come after all this time I am still unable to look in the mirror and say, 'I love me'?* Well, I finally understand why, and am now able to say that I do love myself.

This is now a new season for me. It is really only the beginning of my story. The Claudette I once knew is gone. The loved woman has only just begun to live.

Call Me Loved

Call me mother, call me friend,
Call me sister, for that is who I am.
Call me daughter, call me wife, call me loved –
Not just what you like.

What do I hear you say?
She is one who is lame.
Do you call me names,
My soul and mind profane?
Do you spitefully use the label I've been given
And talk about me, a slave that's driven
By words, by hate, by fear, by loathing
– of self; of him; of her?
But . . .

You can call me mother,
You can call me friend,
Call me sister, for that is who I am.
Call me His daughter, call me his wife,
Call me Loved of God – for I have Life!

Useful Organizations

Anorexia and Bulimia Care
Providence House
The Borough
Wedmore
Somerset
BS28 4EG
Tel: 03000 11 12 13
Parent helpline: Option 1
Sufferer helpline: Option 2
Office: Option 3
Email: mail@anorexiabulimiacare.org.uk
Web: www.anorexiabulimiacare.org.uk

Bullying UK
Headquarters
CAN Mezzanine
49–51 East Road
London
N1 6AH
Tel: 0808 800 2222
Email: parentsupport@familylives.org.uk
Web: www.bullying.co.uk

Diabetes UK Central Office
Macleod House
10 Parkway
London
NW1 7AA
Tel: 020 7424 1000
Email: info@diabetes.org.uk
Web: www.diabetes.org.uk

Mind
15–19 Broadway
Stratford
London
E15 4BQ
Tel: 020 8519 2122
Email: contact@mind.org.uk
Web: www.mind.org.uk

Mind Cymru
3rd Floor, Quebec House
Castlebridge
5–19 Cowbridge Road East
Cardiff
CF11 9AB
Tel: 029 2039 5123
Email: contactwales@mind.org.uk
Web: www.mind.org.uk/mind_cymru

For more information on Claudette visit
w.w.w.claudetteschlitter.com

Authentic

We trust you enjoyed reading this book from
Authentic Media. If you want to be informed of
any new titles from this author and other exciting
releases you can sign up to the Authentic
newsletter online:

www.authenticmedia.co.uk
Contact us
By Post: Authentic Media
52 Presley Way
Crownhill
Milton Keynes
MK8 0ES

E-mail: info@authenticmedia.co.uk

Follow us: